Short-Term
Existential Intervention
in Clinical Practice

Also Available from Lyceum Books, Inc.

Advisory Editor: Thomas M. Meenaghan, *New York University*

A PRACTICAL GUIDE TO SOCIAL SERVICE EVALUATION,
by Carl F. Brun

ENDINGS IN CLINICAL PRACTICE:
EFFECTIVE CLOSURE IN DIVERSE SETTINGS, 2E,
by Joseph Walsh, foreword by Thomas M. Meenaghan

SECONDARY TRAUMATIC STRESS AND THE CHILD
WELFARE PROFESSIONAL,
by Josephine G. Pryce, Kimberly K. Shackelford, and David H. Pryce

STRAIGHT TALK ABOUT PROFESSIONAL ETHICS,
by Kim Strom-Gottfried

WHAT IS PROFESSIONAL SOCIAL WORK?,
By Malcolm Payne

USING STATISTICAL METHODS IN SOCIAL WORK PRACTICE WITH SPSS,
by Soleman H. Abu-Bader

EVIDENCE-BASED PRACTICES FOR SOCIAL WORKERS,
by Thomas O'Hare

USING EVIDENCE IN SOCIAL WORK PRACTICE:
BEHAVIORAL PERSPECTIVES,
by Harold E. Briggs and Tina L. Rzepnicki

CLINICAL ASSESSMENT FOR SOCIAL WORKERS:
QUALITATIVE AND QUANTITATIVE METHODS, 2E,
edited by Catheleen Jordan and Cynthia Franklin

ETHICS IN END-OF-LIFE DECISIONS FOR SOCIAL WORK PRACTICE,
by Ellen Csikai and Elizabeth Chaiten

TEAMWORK IN MULTIPROFESSIONAL CARE,
by Malcolm Payne, foreword by Thomas M. Meenaghan

ADVOCACY PRACTICE FOR SOCIAL JUSTICE,
by Richard Hoefer

Short-Term Existential Intervention in Clinical Practice

Jim Lantz

Joseph Walsh
Virginia Commonwealth University

LYCEUM
BOOKS, INC.

Chicago, Illinois

© Lyceum Books, Inc., 2007

Published by

LYCEUM BOOKS, INC.
5758 S. Blackstone Ave.
Chicago, Illinois 60637
773+643-1903 (Fax)
773+643-1902 (Phone)
lyceum@lyceumbooks.com
http://www.lyceumbooks.com

10 9 8 7 6 5 4 3 2 1

ISBN-13: 978-1-933478-08-1

Library of Congress Cataloging-in-Publication Data

Lantz, James E., 1943–2003
    Short-term existential intervention in clinical practice / Jim Lantz, Joseph Walsh.
        p. ; cm.
    Includes bibliographical references and index.
    ISBN-13: 978-1-933478-08-1(alk. paper)
    1. Existential psychology. 2. Existential psychotherapy. 3. Psychiatry. I. Walsh, Joseph (Joseph F.) II. Title.
    [DNLM: 1. Psychotherapy, Brief—methods. 2. Crisis Intervention—methods.
    3. Existentialism. WM 420.5.P5 L297s 2007]
    BF204.5.S5667 2007
    150.19'2—dc22

                                                    2006103409

To Jan Lantz, who is my love, my wife, and my best friend
—*Jim Lantz*

To my lifelong friend Tom Nangle, who first got me thinking
about existential issues in the ninth grade
—*Joe Walsh*

Contents

PART I: CONCEPTS

FIGURES AND TABLES

Figures

Tables

Preface

Joseph Walsh

CLINICAL PRACTITIONERS FROM THE PROFESSIONS OF SOCIAL WORK, psychology, counseling, nursing, pastoral care, and medicine have increasingly tried to work with the "whole person" over the past thirty years. Members of those professions at one time tended to limit their focus to the client's biological, psychological, and, at times, social selves. Developments in the human services professions since the 1960s have clarified, however, that comprehensive intervention with people who experience a range of emotional problems is only possible with a broad understanding of human functioning. In my own profession of social work this is known as the "person-in-environment" perspective or, more recently, the "biopsychosocial" perspective on human functioning.

Many human service professionals have acknowledged the importance of clients' spiritual, or existential, functioning as it pertains to their experience of problems and solutions. Issues related to purpose in life, sense of meaning in life, ultimate values, and ultimate goals are fundamental to human existence, and yet they have only recently begun to routinely fall within the "appropriate" purview of clinical practitioners. Jim Lantz was a major exception to this recent trend because, like relatively few others, he placed issues pertaining to life's purposes at the forefront of his existential intervention methods beginning in the early 1970s.

Jim's short-term existential intervention orientation is concerned with the potential for emotional problems to damage and disrupt human beings at the spiritual as well as physical, psychological, and social dimensions of existence. Short-term existential intervention is also concerned with the human being's ability to react, deal, and cope with problem situations in a way that results in transcendence and developmental progression.

The approach to short-term existential intervention presented in this book uses relationship, action, and reflection activities to facilitate the development of the four intervention themes of the client's holding, telling, mastering, and honoring. This intervention approach has been developed and refined over the past thirty years and has been found to be effective in single subject and field study research efforts in child welfare, family service, hospital, mental health, settlement house, emergency room, and private practice settings.

Jim Lantz died in 2003, but this book is far more than a tribute to his practice legacy. My own specialization as a long-time clinical practitioner has combined primarily "here and now" psychodynamic interventions with contemporary models of case management, which attend to the biological, psychological, and social aspects of life. I have used (and written extensively about) a clinical case management intervention approach with clients traditionally considered to have serious mental illnesses such as schizophrenia, bipolar disorder, depression, post-traumatic stress disorder, personality disorders, and other diagnoses that can significantly compromise one's ability to achieve life goals. I have always made attention to my clients' spiritual concerns part of my work, although my efforts were not as refined as Jim's own.

This book represents my effort not merely to finish a work that Jim started before his death, but to bring it up to date with the integration of contemporary short-term intervention and case management activities, as well as practice applications across diverse types of clients.

Jim Lantz and I both lived and worked in central Ohio for many years (although I moved away in 1993). We actually worked at two of the same mental health treatment facilities, though not at the same time. While I knew Jim and was influenced by his work, we were never close friends or associates. (I was much closer to his wife, Jan, with whom I worked for several years, and who remains one of the most effective mental health practitioners I have ever known.) Jim and I did have numerous conversations, however, about the nature of clinical practice, and the importance of attending to the whole person, no matter how high or low functioning the person might be. For my part, I resisted trends in the 1990s, initiated by the county mental health board, to turn over the care of low-functioning people with serious mental illness to case managers who had little experience in psychotherapy and relationship development, and who were instead being asked to serve as "service brokers" for their clients. I believed that such efforts to focus only on basic needs were both unethical and doomed to failure, because, as I noted earlier, issues of meaning and purpose are central to the lives of all people.

What is presented in this book, then, is an approach to clinical intervention for use with clients who experience a variety of emotional problems that attends to their biology, psychology, social life, and meaning and purpose issues. It is my belief that there is still far too little attention in clinical practice given to these existential issues, and that this area of practice is likely to become more prominent in the coming years. This book also focuses on short-term intervention, given the present-day realities of external funding that set limits on the amount of contact that many clients can have with their treatment providers.

◆◆◆

Short-Term Existential Intervention for Clinical Practice is divided into two parts. Part 1 contains six chapters that present theoretical material related to the nature and experience of crisis, environmental modification strategies, the principles of existential intervention, the nature of "vicious circles" (patterns of problematic problem-solving), and cross-cultural concerns in existential practice. The nine chapters in part 2 attend to applications of the intervention approach with various client populations. The final chapter considers issues related to the evaluation of short-term existential intervention. The book is filled with clinical illustrations that bring the concepts and interventions to life for the reader.

I should emphasize that the approaches to intervention described in this book do not easily lend themselves to recent trends in the human services toward evidence-based practice. Both Jim and I were/are convinced that the "person" of the practitioner is always highly significant to how well an intervention is provided. Intervention must always be individualized rather than generalized, because it unfolds in the content of the unique relationship between the practitioner and client.

The content of this book is based on each of the authors' thirty-plus years of practice experiences in child welfare, family service, hospital, community mental health, clubhouse, settlement house, homeless shelter, and private practice settings, as well as our years of university teaching experience. This book is written primarily for graduate students in social work, psychology, counseling, nursing, pastoral care, and medicine, and also for more seasoned practitioners who are looking for new ideas about the process and practice of existential intervention that might energize their work.

ACKNOWLEDGMENTS

This book could not have been written without the encouragement and support of my family, friends, students, teachers, and clients. A special word of thanks should go to Ernest Andrews, Richard Boettcher, Sam Dixon, Pat Early, Bill Eldridge, David Follmer, Viktor Frankl, Tom and Libby Gomia, Tom Gregoire, Karen Harper, Mary Ellen Kondrat, Jan Lantz, Max Lantz, Tom Meenaghan, Joe Quaranta, Tony Tripodi, and Linda Welch.

Jim Lantz

I would like to thank Jan Lantz and David Follmer for providing me with the wonderful opportunity to participate in the writing of this book.

Joe Walsh

Part I

Concepts

1

The Nature of Existential Crisis

THIS IS NOT A BOOK ABOUT CRISIS INTERVENTION, BUT IN STUDYING short-term existential intervention, it is important to emphasize the ways in which a person's basic purposes in life may be threatened by any type of emotional problem situation. For this reason we begin with a review of the nature of crisis, with a special consideration of the ways in which many clients experience an existential crisis when they face a variety of internal, interpersonal, and resource problems. Later chapters will focus specifically on how short-term existential intervention builds on these ideas.

A *crisis* can be defined as the perception or experience of an event (genuine harm, the threat of harm, or a challenge) as an intolerable difficulty (James & Gilliland, 2001). The crisis is an aberration from the person's typical pattern of functioning, and he or she cannot manage the event through usual methods of coping. The person either lacks knowledge about how to manage the situation or, due to feeling overwhelmed, lacks the ability to focus his or her energies on it. All people experience crises at times in their lives. A crisis often results when we face a serious stressor with which we have no prior experience. The stressor may be biological (a major illness), interpersonal (the sudden loss of a loved one), or environmental (unemployment or a natural disaster). The Chinese characters that represent the word *crisis* include the one that means danger and another that means opportunity. From this point of view, a crisis can be defined as a "dangerous opportunity." An existential crisis is dangerous because it often feels overwhelming, but it is an opportunity because it often forces us to look for strengths, meanings, and solutions that are outside of our normal range of awareness.

ORIGINS OF CRISIS THEORY

Over the last forty years many definitions of a crisis situation have been proposed, as well as an equally large number of descriptions of *crisis intervention* (Dixon, 1979; Ell, 1996; Frankl, 2000; Greene, 1996; Wolberg, 1965). In some definitions a crisis is considered to be any emergency situation. In other definitions a crisis is considered to be an emergency, but an emergency is not always considered a crisis. In some approaches to crisis intervention the crisis approach is always short term, and in other crisis orientations intervention can be appropriately provided over a short or a longer period of time.

Social workers have practiced crisis intervention since the profession's earliest years (Golan, 1978). In fact, the social work profession emerged in response to socially identified needs to help growing numbers of citizens who experienced high-stress situations. Smith College offered its first summer program in 1918 to train workers in skills for rehabilitating shell-shocked soldiers. Social workers also provided services in the first suicide prevention center, the National Save-a-Life League in New York City, in 1906. Through the years caseworkers assisted families experiencing disruption during the Great Depression; homeless, runaway, and impoverished people (through the Traveler's Aid Societies); and people dealing with life disruptions during World War II (through family service agencies). Social workers generally preferred long-term interventions during those years, but as caseloads and waiting lists increased, they effectively adopted short-term approaches as well (Parad, 1965).

Formal crisis theory was developed in the fields of psychiatry, psychology, and sociology. It first emerged during the 1940s, primarily through the work of psychiatrists Erich Lindemann and Gerald Caplan, both of whom had been affiliated with Massachusetts General Hospital (Roberts, 2000). Lindemann and his associates developed concepts of crisis intervention in the aftermath of Boston's Coconut Grove nightclub fire, in which 493 people died. Their ideas were based on observations of the grief reactions of survivors and the friends and relatives of those who died. Lindemann identified common crisis (grief) reactions of somatic distress, guilt, anger, disrupted patterns of conduct, and preoccupation with images of the deceased. He concluded that the length and outcome of a grief reaction was dependent on the person's having time to mourn, to adjust to the changed environment, and to eventually develop new relationships.

Military psychiatrists have always tried to predict the behavior of soldiers in field situations, and to quickly rehabilitate those who become overwhelmed. Lindemann's ideas were adapted to military intervention methods during World War II. Crisis outcomes were found to be most positive when soldiers were treated close to the setting of the precipitating event (the front lines), when the psychiatrist focused only on the immediate situation, and when the soldier was returned to the combat situation in a relatively short time (Golan, 1978).

Caplan (1990) expanded on Lindemann's work in the 1940s and 1950s. His ideas were influenced by his work with immigrant mothers and children. Among his major contributions to crisis theory was the idea that all people are vulnerable to crisis reactions during developmental transitions, such as moving into adolescence and adulthood. Caplan specified two types of crises: normal life transitions and hazardous events. He was the first to relate the concept of homeostasis to crisis intervention and to describe stages of a crisis reaction, which will be presented later. It is noteworthy that developmental theorists such as Erikson (1968) also postulated the normalcy of psychosocial crises in human development at this time. Further, the field of sociology made important contributions to crisis theory with studies on the effects of stressful family events such as marriage, parenthood, and old age on family structure and member interaction.

In the 1960s the social worker Lydia Rapoport wrote about the importance of adapting various clinical intervention modalities to crisis intervention such as ego psychology and learning theory. She emphasized the importance of rapid assessment and the practitioner's ready access to the victim. Later, Naomi Golan (1978) emphasized that people were most receptive to receiving help during the most difficult period of a crisis, and that intensive, brief interventions were more successful when the client was motivated in this way.

The suicide prevention movement arose in the 1960s, initially with telephone hotlines. Between 1966 and 1972 the number of these centers grew from twenty-eight to almost two hundred. The greatest boost to crisis intervention programs came with the community mental health movement, for which twenty-four-hour crisis programs were a required component. The number of centers with these units grew to almost eight hundred by 1980.

Social interest in providing crisis intervention services exploded during the 1970s for two major reasons (Myer, 2001). One was the increase in geographic mobility in the United States and other modern countries, and many people's subsequent lack of ties to nuclear families and other primary supports. Myer cites evidence of 130 million situational crisis episodes occurring annually in the United States. A second reason is the awareness in science of links between psychological trauma and long-term neurological disorders (Nelson & Carver, 1998). Today, crisis programs continue to be found in mental health centers and hospitals. Most social workers receive training in crisis intervention in schools or their agencies, as it is recognized that clients of all types may experience crises.

Today, crisis intervention can be used with a range of presenting problems such as sexual assault, medical illness, combat stress, post-traumatic stress, migration, suicidal ideation, chemical dependence, personal loss, school violence, partner violence, and family stress (James & Gilliland, 2001). It represents a strengths approach because it underscores the possibility of client growth even in horrible situations. The social worker must build upon clients' strengths in order to help them adapt to, and grow from, the experience.

In this book a clinical situation will be considered to be a crisis if and when an individual, couple, or family develops a significant disruption in physical, psychosocial, or spiritual functioning following both a history of adequate functioning and the occurrence of a crisis-triggering event or events (Lantz, 1978; Lindemann, 1944; Wolberg, 1965). This type of crisis is illustrated in figure 1.1.

Figure 1.1 The nature of crisis.

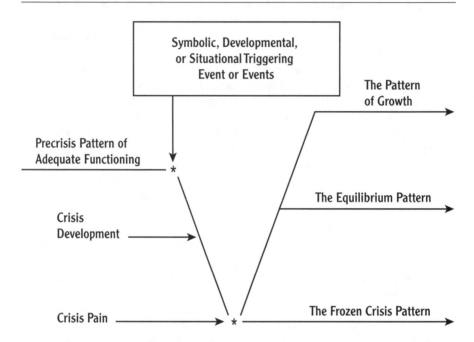

MAJOR CONCEPTS IN CRISIS THEORY

While this book presents a unique approach to existential intervention, it is useful to present several major ideas that are generally considered to be important to the practitioner's understanding of crisis situations.

Stress

Stress can be defined as an event in which environmental or internal demands tax or exceed a person's coping resources (Lazarus & Lazarus, 1994). The event may be *biological* (a disturbance in body systems, such as the experience of a disease), *psychological* (cognitive and emotional factors involved in the evaluation of a stressor, such as the fear of an important relationship ending), *social* (the disruption of a social unit; for example, the closing of a town's major industrial plant), or *existential* (a threat to one's sense of meaning or purpose). Stress can be summarized into three categories (Rapoport, 1965):

1. *Harm* refers to the effects of a damaging event that has already occurred.
2. *Threat* is probably the most common form of psychological and existential stress, in that the person perceives a potential for harm in an event that has not yet happened.

3. *Challenge* consists of events that a person appraises as opportunities rather than occasions for alarm. The person is mobilized to struggle against the obstacle, as with a threat, but with a different attitude. Faced with a threat, a person is likely to act defensively. In a state of challenge the person is excited and confident about the task to be undertaken. The challenge may be perceived as a productive experience.

The nature of a person's experience of stress is related to biological constitution and previous experiences in managing stress (Aldwin, 1994). Vulnerability to stress is also related to one's position in the social structure, with some social positions (including poverty, racism, and blocked opportunities) exposed to a greater number of adverse situations than others (Lupien, King, Meaney, & McEwen, 2000). Although a single event may pose a crisis for one person but not another, some stressors are so severe that they are almost universally experienced as crises.

Traumatic stress refers to events that involve actual or threatened severe injury or death to oneself or to significant others (APA, 2000). These include *natural* (such as flood, tornado, earthquake) and *technological* (such as nuclear) disasters; *war and related problems;* and *individual* traumas, such as being raped or assaulted (Aldwin, 1994). Many trauma survivors experience a set of symptoms known as post-traumatic stress disorder (PTSD; APA, 2000). These symptoms include persistent reliving of the traumatic event, persistent avoidance of stimuli associated with the traumatic event, and a persistently high state of arousal. The symptoms of PTSD may occur as soon as one week after the event, and as much as thirty years afterward. Complete or partial recovery from symptoms is possible but not certain (almost 50% of survivors continue to experience some long-term symptoms), which supports the importance of timely professional intervention (Sadock & Sadock, 2003).

Crisis

The term *crisis* was defined earlier. To elaborate, the experience of crisis occurs in three stages (Caplan, 1990). First, there is a sharp and sudden increase in the person's level of tension. Second, the person tries but fails to cope with the stress, which further increases tension and contributes to the sense of being overwhelmed. At this point the person is highly receptive to accepting help. Third, within approximately four weeks the crisis resolves, either negatively (with an unhealthy coping solution) or positively (with successful management of the crisis and perhaps an enhanced sense of personal competence). The emotions most likely to emerge in a person's experience of crisis include anxiety, guilt, shame, sadness, envy, jealousy, and disgust (Lazarus, 1993).

TYPES OF CRISES

Crises can be classified into three types. *Developmental* crises occur as events in the normal flow of life create dramatic changes that produce extreme responses.

Examples include the birth of one's child, college graduation, a midlife career change, and retirement from work. People may experience these types of crises if they have difficulty negotiating the typical challenges outlined by Erikson (1968) and Germain and Gitterman (1996). *Situational* crises refer to uncommon and extraordinary events that a person has no way of forecasting or controlling. Examples include physical injuries, sexual assault, loss of a job, illness, and the death of a loved one. *Existential* crises are characterized by escalating inner conflicts related to issues of purpose in life, responsibility, independence, freedom, and commitment. Examples include remorse over past life choices, a feeling that one's life has no meaning, and a questioning of one's basic values or spiritual beliefs.

A PERSON'S RESPONSE TO A CRISIS

A client in crisis may follow three general courses (James & Gilliland, 2001). In the *growth* pattern the client recovers from the event and then, often with the help of a practitioner, develops new skills and strengths. In the *equilibrium* pattern the client returns to the precrisis level of functioning but does not experience enhanced social functioning. In the *frozen crisis* pattern the client does not improve but makes adjustments that involve harmful strategies (such as substance abuse) that keep him or her in a chronically troubled state. Whether a stress experience becomes a crisis depends on the person's coping capacities, so we now turn to a discussion of that concept.

Coping and Adaptation

Coping is a person's efforts to master the demands of stress (Lazarus, 1993). It consists of the thoughts, feelings, and actions that constitute those efforts. *Adaptation* involves related adjustments the person makes in biological responses, perceptions, or lifestyle.

Biological Coping

The biological view of stress and coping emphasizes the body's attempts to maintain physical equilibrium, or a steady state of functioning (Seyle, 1991). Stress results from any demand on the body, specifically the nervous and hormonal systems, during perceived emergencies. The body's response to a stressor is called the *general adaptation syndrome.* It occurs in three stages. In the state of *alarm,* the body becomes aware of a threat. During *resistance* the body attempts to maintain or restore homeostasis. This is an active response of the body in which endorphins and specialized cells of the immune system fight off stress and infection. In the third stage, *exhaustion,* the body terminates coping efforts because of its inability to physically sustain the state of disequilibrium. The immune system is constructed for adaptation to stress, but the cumulative wear and tear of stress episodes can gradually deplete its resources. Common outcomes of chronic stress include stomach and intestinal disorders, high blood pressure, heart problems, and some emotional disorders.

Psychological Coping

The psychological aspect of managing stress can be viewed in two different ways. Some theorists consider coping ability to be a stable personality characteristic, or *trait;* others see it instead as a transient *state*—a process that changes over time depending on the context (Lazarus, 1993). Those who consider coping to be a trait see it as an acquired defensive style, a set of automatic responses that enable us to minimize perceived threats. Those who see coping as a state, or process, observe that coping strategies change depending on our perceptions of the threats. The context has an impact on our perceived and actual abilities to apply effective coping mechanisms. The trait and state approaches can be combined. That is, coping can be conceptualized as a general pattern of managing stress that incorporates flexibility across diverse contexts.

A person's coping efforts may be *problem focused* or *emotion focused* (Lazarus, 1993). The function of problem-focused coping, which includes confrontation and problem-solving strategies, is to change the stressful situation. This method tends to dominate when the person views the situation as controllable by action. In emotion-focused coping (distancing, avoidance, and reappraisal of the threat), the external situation does not change, but the person's behavior or attitudes change with respect to it. When a person views stressful conditions as unchangeable, emotion-focused coping may dominate. People may productively use either of these general approaches at different times.

American culture tends to venerate problem-focused coping and the independently functioning self, and to distrust emotion-focused coping and what may be called relational coping. Relational coping takes into account actions that maximize the survival of others—such as families, children, and friends—as well as the self (Banyard & Graham-Bermann, 1993). Feminist theorists propose that women are more likely than men to employ the relational coping strategies of negotiation and forbearance. Further, power imbalances and social forces such as racism and sexism affect the coping strategies of individuals. Practitioners must be careful not to assume that one type of coping is superior to the other.

People exhibit some similarities between the ways in which they cope with crises and the ways in which they cope with everyday stress, but there are also differences (Aldwin, 1994). Because people tend to have less control in crisis situations, a primary coping strategy is emotional numbing, or the constriction of emotional expression. They also make greater use of the defense mechanism of denial. Confiding in others takes on greater importance. The process of coping takes a longer time, and reactions may be delayed for months. The search for ultimate values and life meanings takes on greater importance, and personal identity transformations are more common. Despite the many negative consequences of traumatic stress, however it is important to recognize that survivors sometimes report the experience as one that is positive. In this growth pattern clients utilize their experience to discover new strengths, skills, behavioral patterns, insights, and meaning potentials in their lives.

As described next, a strong system of social support helps a person to avoid or recover from crises and other problem situations.

Social Support

Social support can be defined as the interpersonal interactions and relationships that provide people with assistance or positive feelings of attachment (Hobfoll, Freedy, Lane, & Geller, 1990). A key function of crisis intervention should involve the client's linkage with formal or natural social support resources. (The topic of formal support is addressed in detail in chapter 2.) The utilization of natural supports by clients is important because of limits in the scope and availability of formal services. Most importantly, natural supports promote normalcy in clients' lives.

There are many possible indicators of social support. Examples include the client's subjective perceptions of support from family and friends (Procidano & Heller, 1983) and the availability of others who can provide listening, task appreciation, task challenge, emotional support, emotional challenge, reality confirmation, and personal assistance (Richman, Rosenfeld, & Hardy, 1993). One relatively simple system with utility for crisis intervention focuses on the availability of *material* support (food, clothing, shelter, and other concrete items), *emotional* support (all interpersonal supports), and *instrumental* support (services provided by casual contacts, such as grocers, hairstylists, and landlords) (Walsh & Connelly, 1996). Supportive relationships often occur in clusters, distinct categories of interaction such as the nuclear family, extended family, friends, neighbors, formal community relationships, school peers, work peers, church associates, recreational groups, and professional associations (Vaux, 1990). Having contacts in a variety of clusters is desirable, as it indicates that a person is supported in many areas of life.

How Social Support Aids Coping

The experience of emotional stress creates an emotional arousal in a person that reduces the efficiency of his or her cognitive functioning (Caplan, 1990). When under stress, a person becomes less effective at focusing attention and negotiating the environment. Social supports help to compensate for these deficits by nurturing and promoting an ordered worldview, promoting hope, promoting timely withdrawal and initiative, providing guidance, providing a communication channel with the social world, affirming personal identity, providing material help, containing distress through reassurance and affirmation, ensuring adequate rest, and mobilizing other personal supports.

There is no consensus about how practitioners can evaluate a client's level of social support, but one useful model suggests gathering information in three areas

(Vaux, 1988). The practitioner asks the client to list all the people with whom he or she has interacted in the past one or two weeks. Next, the practitioner asks the client to draw from that list the people he or she perceives to be supportive in significant ways. The client is then asked to describe specific recent acts of support provided by those individuals. Finally, the practitioner asks the client to evaluate the adequacy of the support received from each source. Based on this assessment, the practitioner can identify the client's supports and target certain areas for development.

HISTORY OF ADEQUATE FUNCTIONING

In a crisis situation the individual, couple, or family has usually had a lengthy period of adequate human functioning prior to the onset of the problem (Dixon, 1979; Whitaker, 1989). That is, the client experiencing the crisis has functioned well in the past and has demonstrated strengths, capacities, and resiliencies in a variety of difficult situations. The period of adequate functioning prior to the development of the crisis is proof of the crisis client's capacities and strengths (Golan, 1978). His or her strengths are the very reason that intervention can often be brief, short term, time limited, and growth oriented.

THE TRIGGERING EVENT

In a problem situation, the individual, couple, or family's experience of a significant disruption in physical, psychosocial, or spiritual functioning follows the occurrence of a significant triggering event or events (Berger, 1984). At times this is a situational event such as a car accident, death of a loved one, development of a physical disease, divorce, fire, rape, tornado, or loss of one's job. At other times the triggering event can be a life stage change such as the birth of a child, getting married, a young adult leaving home for either work or college, or an older adult who loses his or her aging partner to death. Although the triggering event is most frequently a specific, concrete, and fairly obvious situation or difficulty, sometimes the event is more difficult to identify, because it is subtle and perhaps symbolic (Greene & Lee, 2002). One example of a symbolic event that led to a crisis is described here:

> Mr. Jackson is an African American combat veteran who developed panic attacks, crying spells, and depression shortly after his son turned thirteen years old. Mr. Jackson was a Gulf Storm combat veteran who had made an excellent adjustment on a surface level when he returned home from the Middle East. In Mr. Jackson's crisis situation, his son's thirteenth birthday stimulated his memory of a combat event that he had repressed for many years. His son's birthday helped him to remember that in combat he had killed a young soldier who was about the age of his son. Mr. Jackson's recovery of this combat memory stimulated a crisis. He had not worked through the original painful event but had instead repressed it. After many years of repression and apparent adequate functioning, Mr. Jackson developed a crisis shortly after his son's birthday. In this situation the symbolic crisis event gave Mr. Jackson a new opportunity to work through his pain and feelings of guilt about a horrible combat experience.

CRISIS PAIN

Crisis pain is an individual, couple, or family's negative emotional reaction to the occurrence of a stressful and difficult triggering event (Lantz, 1978; Walsh, 2003). When crisis pain is greater than the person's ability to tolerate and process the pain, the person will use defense methods to cover or cloud the experience of crisis pain (Lantz & Gyamerah, 2002; Walsh, 2000). Defense mechanisms that are frequently utilized by people in crisis pain include avoidance, dependency, and aggression; these can also be understood more positively as coping mechanisms (Lantz, 1978, 2000; Yalom, 1980). These three defense methods protect the person from awareness of his or her crisis pain but also disrupt the person's ability to work through the crisis pain at the physical, psychosocial, and spiritual dimensions of existence (Lantz, 2001; Lantz & Gregoire, 2003; Wolberg, 1965).

HUMAN RESPONSES TO THE CRISIS SITUATION

There are three basic patterns of response that people manifest after they experience a crisis-triggering event, crisis pain, and their own use of defense mechanisms. These include the patterns (introduced earlier) of growth, equilibrium, and frozen crisis, or continuous dysfunction. These three patterns include behavior at the physical, psychosocial, and spiritual dimensions of existence (Frankl, 1969, 2001; see figure 1.1).

The Growth Pattern

In the growth pattern the individual, couple, or family initially demonstrates deterioration in functioning in response to the crisis situation (Dixon, 1979; Wolberg, 1965). After this initial period of deterioration and despair, the client or client system is able to find a way not only to return to the previous level of functioning, but to move beyond it. That is, they utilize their crisis experience to discover new strengths, skills, behavioral patterns, ways of thinking, insights, and meaning potentials in their lives. They are able to grow and develop in a way that is even more effective than before their crisis experience (Greene, 1996; Grove & Burnaugh, 2002; Lantz & Gomia, 1995; Walsh, 1999). The primary intervention goal in short-term existential intervention is to help the client turn his or her experience of crisis into an experience of growth and "becoming" as rapidly as is safely possible (Frankl, 1975; Lantz, 2000; Lantz & Gyamerah, 2002; Walsh, 2003).

The Equilibrium Pattern

In the equilibrium pattern the person or people in crisis initially demonstrate a deterioration in functioning following the triggering event. The client system is able to respond to the crisis by eventually returning to their precrisis level of functioning, but they are not able to utilize the experience in a way that results in growth and improved functioning (Frankl, 1978; Lantz, 2000; Lantz & Thorward, 1985; Walsh, 2003). In the equilibrium pattern little or no growth occurs in the life of the client and, at times, much time and effort are required to return to an equilibrium state. Again, the primary treatment goal is to help the client find a way to turn the crisis experience into a process of growth rather than simply to return to the equilibrium state (Frankl, 1978; Lantz, 2002).

The Frozen Crisis Pattern

In the frozen crisis pattern the client system also demonstrates a long-term pattern of adequate functioning prior to the occurrence of a triggering event, and then a deterioration of functioning at the physical, psychosocial, and spiritual dimensions of existence (Lantz, 1978; Wolberg, 1965). What is different about this pattern is that the client does not rebound or return to either a growth pattern or an equilibrium pattern. In the frozen pattern the client stays in the dysfunctional pattern and may stay frozen for years. The client system's response to the triggering event or events is a long-term pattern of dysfunctional behavior that crystallizes into a consistent pattern of depression, anxiety, and despair. Many clients who are diagnosed as traumatized (PTSD) or as having a personality disorder are in a frozen crisis pattern. In working with this type of client, the goal is to disturb the long-term pattern of dysfunctional behavior and to help the person develop into a growth-pattern client (Frankl, 1997, 2000; Lantz, 1978, 2000; Yalom, 1980). It is important to take a thorough social history to identify past strengths in this crisis situation, and to utilize a strengths perspective even when the client is functioning poorly.

THE PRACTICE SITUATION

Although the goal of the practitioner in short-term existential intervention is to help the client or client system turn the crisis from a process of pain and despair into a process of growth and becoming, mental health funding sources such as insurance agencies, private charity organizations, and government funding and planning boards are not always so comprehensive in their thinking about what is possible. In many situations, funding sources only desire that the crisis client return to a pattern of equilibrium in as short a time as possible. These funding sources do not generally believe that they have an obligation to fund a growth-centered intervention approach (Lantz, 2000). This is unfortunate for clients in crisis and for society at large. Every crisis situation provides considerable opportunity for the client in crisis to find new solutions, new patterns, new meanings, and new opportunities to become more complete than he or she has been in the past (Berg & Dolan, 2001). When a client is helped to consider and take advantage of these opportunities, he or she is much more likely to avoid crises and other types of significant problems in living in the future.

Every practitioner must decide whether or not he or she is willing to focus on equilibrium work or will attempt to help clients develop new patterns of growth. This is a clinical but also a moral decision that must be faced in every situation where a client requests help and must rely on some form of external funding to pay for the intervention (Lantz, 2000). It is more ethically sound to try to help every client reach the maximum of his or her potential by turning a crisis into a pattern of growth.

SUMMARY

In this first chapter a number of important concepts have been presented, including the nature of crisis, the origins of crisis theory, and the human response to crisis situations. The short-term existential intervention approach can properly be called both a strengths perspective and an existential approach. Short-term existential intervention represents a strengths approach because it believes in the real possibility of client growth even in horrible situations and because the practitioner must be able to identify client strengths in order to help them change. It is also an existential approach in that the practitioner must be able to fully hear the client's pain in an empathic way. With this level of understanding, the client can use the practitioner's support in a way that facilitates change (Lantz & Lantz, 2001).

The next chapter discusses the importance of environmental modification in existential intervention. The remaining chapters in part 1 present the nature of short-term existential intervention.

2

Environmental Modification in Short-Term Existential Intervention: Clinical Case Management

ENVIRONMENTAL MODIFICATION IS A MAJOR FACTOR IN THE ACTUALIZATION of therapeutic opportunities for clients experiencing emotional problems. In many instances the loss of external supports and resources is the primary reason why problems develop, and far too often the absence of such supports is the reason why a problem evolves into a frozen pattern of despair (Dixon, 1979; Lantz, 1978). As a result, environmental modification skills are often the most important skills that an existential practitioner can possess (Lantz, 1993; Wolberg, 1965). These skills can be summarized as *clinical case management* (Walsh, 2000). Major activities in this type of intervention include linking, advocacy, and activism. Two activities that are utilized less often but are still important are tribalization and the family intervention team approach (Lantz, 1978).

CLINICAL CASE MANAGEMENT

Clinical case management is an approach to human service delivery that integrates elements of clinical social work and environmental modification. The range of needs for clients includes social relationships, housing, income support, medical care, job training, recreation, life skills development, counseling, and medication. In clinical case management the practitioner combines the sensitivity and interpersonal skill of the psychotherapist with the creativity and action orientation of the environmental architect (Surber, 1994).

Clinical case management includes the following eleven activities contained in three areas of focus (Kanter, 1996; Walsh, 2000): engagement, assessment, and planning (the initial phase); linking with community resources, consulting with families and caregivers, maintaining and expanding social networks, collaboration with physicians and hospitals, and advocacy (the environmental focus); and inter-mittent individual psychotherapy, independent living skills development, and client psychoeducation (the client focus).

TASKS AND ACTIVITIES

The therapeutic tasks of clinical case management practice are as follows (adapted from Harris & Bergman, 1988):

- ◆ Forging a relationship, or making a positive connection with a client. This may unfold in a variety of ways depending on a particular client's character-istics and may range from high levels of interaction to the maintenance of interpersonal formality.
- ◆ Modeling healthy behaviors. When this is successful, the client internalizes an awareness that separate events can be organized into a coherent whole; that action can influence the course of events; that events unfold in a pre-dictable, understandable way; and that he or she has unique needs, goals, and skills.
- ◆ Altering the client's physical environment through processes of creation, facilitation, and adjustment.

THE PRACTITIONER-CLIENT RELATIONSHIP IN CLINICAL CASE MANAGEMENT

The case management relationship is the sustaining link between the client and external world and provides the client with an environment of safety (Sexton & Whiston, 1994). The skills of relationship development in clinical case manage-ment (and short-term existential intervention as well) are summarized as skills of client *sustainment* (Woods & Hollis, 2000). Through the skills of sustainment, the practitioner:

- ◆ Listens actively and sympathetically
- ◆ Conveys a continuing attitude of good will
- ◆ Demonstrates consistency in the relationship
- ◆ Directly expresses confidence or esteem
- ◆ Nonverbally communicates interest, attentiveness
- ◆ Realistically reassures the client about potential for goal achievement
- ◆ Realistically encourages the client to persist
- ◆ Possibly offers environmental support

Sustainment is powerful for the client. It promotes a confiding relationship, in-stills a sense of the practitioner's competence and caring, provides an antidote to alienation, enhances the client's morale and determination to persist, and inspires and maintains the expectation of help. It also creates an atmosphere of trust where confrontation can take place effectively, if necessary. In short, a relationship of sustainment provides a context in which the full range of interventions can be implemented effectively.

CLINICAL SKILLS IN CASE MANAGEMENT

In addition to relationship-building skills, the skills needed for clinical case management include the ability to (Harris & Bergman, 1988; Kanter, 1996, 1995):

- ◆ Make ongoing judgments about the intensity of one's involvement with a client
- ◆ Assess and recognize a client's fluctuating competence and changing needs
- ◆ Titrate support in order to maximize a client's capacity for self-directed behavior
- ◆ Appreciate the effects of social factors on a client's sense of competence
- ◆ Understand how clients both shape and internalize their environments
- ◆ Appreciate a client's conscious and unconscious motives for behavior
- ◆ Develop a longitudinal view of the client's strengths, limitations, and symptoms

With this overview of the components of case management, the major activities involved in the process are now described.

LINKING

Linking is the art of bringing together the resources of different agencies, personnel, volunteer groups, and relevant individuals, and coordinating their efforts on behalf of a client system (Barker, 1999). In linking, the practitioner is expected to have knowledge about human resources that are available to the client and to know how to gain access to such resources. Although not every client requires linking to services, the practitioner's ability to engage in linking often speeds up intervention and can prevent the problem situation from transforming into a frozen pattern of maladaptive behavior (Lantz, 1978).

One example of effective linking is the practitioner's directing a family that has lost its home due to a natural disaster to an agency that provides temporary shelter for homeless families. The practitioner may also link the family with a department of social services to receive income assistance, although the shelter agency may provide that service to its residents. Even if the crisis is primarily due to the housing issue, the practitioner's activities may also include counseling as the family members adjust and cope with the disruptive situation.

ADVOCACY

Advocacy in short-term existential intervention can be defined as a process of directly representing and defending clients, of championing clients' rights, and of facilitating client empowerment (Barker, 1999). Advocacy is a basic obligation of the helping professions. When taking on the advocate role, the practitioner speaks out on behalf of the client to bring about changes in the environment that contributes to the client's difficulties.

An example of basic advocacy is the practitioner's contacting an agency where the client has been seeking job training assistance but has been denied services or kept on a waiting list for an inappropriate length of time. It is not uncommon for bureaucratic procedures to keep a client from receiving such services, and the practitioner, who should understand the service system more fully than the client and may have personal contacts at the agency, may call or visit the agency on the client's behalf to make sure that appropriate services are provided in a timely way. The client's sustained growth may be ensured if the practitioner educates the client about how to become an effective self-advocate.

ACTIVISM

Activism is planned behavior used by the practitioner to achieve social or political objectives through activities such as consciousness-raising, coalition development, publicity, and other actions to enhance social change (Schneider & Lester, 2001). In crisis intervention, activism involves a rejection of the neutral or passive clinical stance in favor of taking specific actions on behalf of the client's well-being. Such actions are generally targeted at creating new resources in a community. Activism can benefit both the practitioner's client and also the clients of other practitioners who need such resources.

An example of social activism is the practitioner's participation in political lobbying to expand the range of rights traditionally accorded to marital couples so that these rights also apply to single persons living together, including gay and lesbian couples. The practitioner may be working with a gay couple that is experiencing financial problems stemming from laws that limit their capacity to share certain financial or resource rights.

The next two activities are less commonly utilized than those described above, but they clearly demonstrate the positive potential of creative approaches to environmental intervention in existential practice.

TRIBALIZATION

Tribalization is a process of social linkage between a client, family members, friends, neighbors, and associates. Tribalization involves strengthening the supportive quality of existing social networks, establishing new social networks, and creating linkages among social networks. This process has sometimes been described as network therapy (Barker, 1999) Tribalization is a method of network intervention that incorporates a positive view of community as a setting in which positive supports can be activated toward the alleviation of private distress. The goal of tribalization is to change a problem situation by mobilizing family members, relatives, friends, and neighbors to meet at the client's home to actively discuss and support constructive, alternative resource and behavioral options for the client. The process is relatively brief once it gets underway, but the planning may be extensive.

There are six major stages in the tribalization process: retribalization, polarization, mobilization for action, depression, impasse breakthrough, and exhaustion and elation (Speck & Attneave, 1973). According to Rueveni (1975), tribalization should not be attempted unless the client is highly motivated to make changes in his or her life. Without the proper level of motivation the client will not be willing to go through the process of helping the worker contact and arrange for a potentially large group of friends, neighbors, and relatives to meet with the client and intervention team at the client's home.

An example of a problem situation in which tribalization might be appropriate is when an adolescent member of a family abruptly begins acting out in dangerous ways (such as drug use and criminal behavior) in response to the death of a parent. The practitioner can organize a variety of family and community people to come together to help the adolescent consider a more constructive way of life. If the client is willing and able to help arrange such a meeting, the network intervention team (comprised of several practitioners involved in the client's care who come together for this purpose only) first helps those network members who are present to begin the *retribalization* process. The team attempts to help the network members get acquainted or reacquainted and develop an awareness of the client's concerns and a sense of network cohesion. In this example, network members may include nuclear family, extended family, several close neighbors, the client's close friends, perhaps several local merchants who have been or might become involved in the client's life, a minister, and a police officer. Network cohesion can be facilitated through a variety of activities such as mingling, focused discussion, singing, and other activities.

The next part of the process is *polarization.* In this stage, the various aspects of the client's conflicts are manifested in front of the network assembly. This is generally done by having the client or family members sit in the middle of the assembly and share with each other and the network members their problems, concerns, and conflicts. During this stage, different members of the assembly usually begin to develop empathy for the family members, and members of the network may take sides with certain family members about an issue. After this has occurred, the network team helps each member of the family develop network support groups. This is done by finding activists within the network who are willing to help particular family members, rather than simply talk about what might be helpful. Network members may offer specific helping activities, resources, and even financial aid to the client in crisis. In the above example, the minister might suggest volunteer activities, a local merchant might suggest structured work, and the police officer might suggest community recreation activities.

The process of finding network activists who are willing to help, and then developing support groups for the various family members, leads into the *mobilization for action* stage. The support groups mount an effort to find and carry out alternative actions that will help the family members break out of the problem situation. In this example, the network members who made suggestions for the misbehaving adolescent may devise specific plans for engaging in their suggested activities. Sometimes such initial attempts may fail (they may be deemed unworkable or may be rejected by the client). If so, the family network may move into a *depression* stage, characterized by feelings of uncertainly about how to constructively proceed.

If the depression stage unfolds, the intervention team helps the network members share their feelings of frustration and concern. The team can often stimulate a breakthrough by leading discussions in the meeting that serve to regenerate energy and positive feelings. This will often lead to a breakthrough of the impasse. The client, family, and network members adopt an acceptable plan of action, and the final stage of *exhaustion and elation* is achieved. In some instances the approach will be considered so helpful by the client and network members that they will decide to continue meeting together, even without the presence of the network intervention team, to expand and continue the gains achieved during the tribalization process. This is not typical, however, and is not necessary for positive changes to be sustained.

FAMILY INTERVENTION TEAM APPROACH

Another form of tribalization is one in which the intervention team itself becomes a network and serves as the external resources for the family in crisis. This approach has been documented as effective with families in poverty who have few external resources, and also in situations resulting from a natural disaster. It was first developed at the Colorado Psychiatric Hospital in Denver (Langsley & Kaplan, 1968). The major goal of the approach is to help people who cannot afford psychiatric hospitalization to receive effective interventions. This is done through an intervention approach that recognizes the family group as a social unit with the resources and capacity to manage and resolve the stress factors involved in the triggering of one member's psychiatric symptoms. It is similar to the idea of case management carried out by a team of practitioners.

The major principles of the family crisis intervention approach include the following:

- ◆ Focusing only on the present illness or problem
- ◆ Enhancing the client's self-esteem
- ◆ Using social and environmental resources extensively
- ◆ Using medications when necessary
- ◆ Leaving an open door for the family to return to treatment after termination (Langsley & Kaplan, 1968).

In the family intervention team approach the family members are seen by at least one team member immediately after the request for service. One reason for the prompt response is that the mere promise of help gives the client and family members hope that there will be some relief from the tension that has become so troublesome.

After providing an immediate service response, the family crisis team is careful to define the present difficulty as one that involves all the family members, so that all members understand the importance of their involvement in the intervention process. Further, the treatment team attempts to get other caregivers from the community involved in the intervention, much like the process described in the previous section. It is not unusual to find ministers, physicians, caseworkers, probation officers, and other community people participating in the intervention. Such community helpers are encouraged and invited to work with the family intervention unit as well as to continue their relationships with the family after the formal intervention has ended.

In the family team approach it is assumed that a recent event has triggered the family's service request and that what is most helpful to the family is a resolution of what is currently troubling the members. Seeing all the family members helps the team develop a better understanding of what has happened to set off the crisis. A primary goal for the intervention is to reduce the level of tension in the family as quickly as possible. This can often be done by defining the psychiatric symptoms as a way the identified client is attempting to communicate his or her concerns to the rest of the family. Specific prescriptions for family behavior change depend on the unique situation of every family group. It is assumed that a state of crisis within the family group signals a change in family equilibrium. After the treatment team has decided, with the family's input, which events have triggered the state of equilibrium change, the team gives each family member a set of specific tasks to carry out that are designed to help the family group regain a state of equilibrium.

Toward the end of intervention there is often an improvement in the identified client, as demonstrated by a reduction in psychiatric symptoms. As this occurs, the focus of intervention changes to include helping the family discover how the behavior of each member (unintentionally) helped to set off the crisis, and how each member can change his or her behavior in a way that may decrease the chance of such a crisis occurring again.

In many instances this type of family intervention helps family members recognize a need for ongoing professional assistance centered on long-term interactional problems. If this happens, the family is referred to another agency for further intervention.

SUMMARY

Resource deficiency is often a major issue in the practice of short-term existential intervention. In this chapter a number of intervention methods have been discussed that can be utilized to enhance resource availability to the client during intervention. These methods include clinical case management featuring activism, linking, advocacy, tribalization, and team intervention.

This chapter closes with a first-person account of a clinical case manager who utilized many of the activities defined in this chapter and who also, near the end of the intervention, participated in a moving tribalization process with his client's family.

THE SPIRITUAL CELEBRATION

I work at an agency that serves juvenile offenders. The agency provides educational services, day treatment, crisis intervention, and intensive home-based services. All the clients have criminal histories and severe emotional disturbances. The courts usually refer the kids to us. All staff provided case management and advocacy services for clients, doing whatever it takes to get them productively involved in their communities. At the same time we have to regularly file reports on their behaviors to the probation officers, which makes for a partially adversarial relationship. Almost all the clients are African American, and I'm the only white worker in the agency.

I work in the home-based program. One of my clients was Eddie, a nineteen-year-old African American male. He had spent the previous five years in a correctional facility for drug trafficking, weapons possession, and manslaughter. He was delivered directly from that facility into our program. I met Eddie along with his probation officer when he arrived home that day. Eddie was quite intimidating to me. He was big, muscular, intense, and sullen. Our relationship seemed to go nowhere for two weeks as I checked on him every day at his home. Eddie did not say a single word to me until I had spent about fourteen hours in his company. His family members, including his grandmother, mother, and three sisters, were more friendly and approachable.

To my astonishment and delight, this turned out to be a successful intervention. During those first few weeks I talked to Eddie a lot in spite of the fact that he never responded. I tried to make him feel comfortable, show respect for his family, and affirm his reluctance to place any trust in me. I talked so much because it made me more anxious not to talk, and I hoped that Eddie would eventually warm up. Finally he did begin to open up, very slowly. He seemed to feel positively about my role. We spent a great deal of time together for the next few months.

Most home-based work is intense, and I probably spent seven hours per week with Eddie. I got to know all his family members very well and shared many meals with them. Eddie turned out to have many strengths, including a desire to turn his life around, and he made great progress. I helped him get his Graduate Equivalency Diploma and his driver's license, and I supported his cooperation with probationary expectations. Best of all, I was able to be a mentor for him. We went to the beach, the movies, to parks, and we did a lot of driving around, always talking about his thoughts and plans.

After several months he was ready to be released from probation. Eddie had met his goals, and his paperwork was nearing completion, but I was concerned about feelings he might be having about our ending. Of course I was concerned about my feelings, too. I wanted to arrange for some type of celebration. I called his grandmother, to whom Eddie and I both felt close, and asked for her thoughts about our ending. She came up with a great idea—a community spiritual gathering in their home.

I had never participated in anything quite like this. The ceremony included Eddie, his grandmother, mother, sisters, and several close friends and relatives. No other professional staff were invited. Eddie's grandmother and I co-led the ceremony, which lasted about ninety minutes. All of us took turns reflecting on Eddie's life up to that point, and we helped him look to his future. Many tears of joy were shed. I read a letter to Eddie in which I summed up my good feeling about our work, and about the journey we had made together. I gave him the letter after I finished. There were frequent references to God and religion in the messages others shared. That was fine!

This was a stirring emotional experience for all of us. I learned that community and spirituality are important parts of the lives of many clients and should never be ignored by professionals. I was also helped to frame all my endings with clients as "new beginnings," as corny as that might sound, because that theme was articulated by many of the guests. I was also reminded in this ceremony that clinical endings often affect more people than the client and professional, and practitioners should consider including some of these other people in their final meetings.

3

Elements of Short-Term Existential Intervention

SHORT-TERM EXISTENTIAL INTERVENTION IS A TREATMENT ORIENTATION for use with individuals, couples, and families who are experiencing emotional or interpersonal problems. It is based on insights from the biopsychosocial understanding of human existence, humanistic psychology, the strengths perspective, psychoanalytic theory, and existential philosophy. In the psychoanalytic context, the imposition and experience of suffering are invaluable components of authenticity and therapeutic change (Guy, 2005). The existential perspective gives recognition to human potential coupled with an awareness of the irreversible difficulties of the human condition (Bretherton & Orner, 2003).

Although existential intervention is generally considered to be a longer-term approach (Lantz, 2000) it can also be utilized effectively as a brief intervention (one to approximately six sessions). When used as a short-term model, existential intervention includes the following characteristics that make it different from the longer-term approach (adapted from Corwin, 2002):

- ◆ Rapid assessment
- ◆ Identification of a limited number of problems for work
- ◆ Client and practitioner agreement on time limitations
- ◆ Clearly defined problems and goals
- ◆ An intervention agreement
- ◆ Focused interventions
- ◆ A session-to-session monitoring of progress

Still, it is important to emphasize that existential intervention is not always short term (Lantz, 2002). Long-term intervention is often appropriate when the client is suffering in a frozen crisis pattern either because short-term intervention has failed or because the client did not receive help immediately after he or she developed a particular problem (Lantz & Gregoire, 2000a, 2000b).

In short-term existential intervention the relationship between the client and practitioner, through the process of sustainment described in the last chapter, is the most important factor in helping the client overcome or master the problem situation. It is the practitioner's responsibility to use the relationship and the intervention process to help the client enrich his or her life at the three "dimensions of existence" that are often disrupted by a problem situation. These dimensions include being "of" the world, "in" the world, and "for" the world (Frankl, 1969; Lantz, 2001).

This chapter outlines the process of short-term existential intervention from the point of view of these three dimensions of existence. Intervention cannot be described as existential unless the practitioner consistently focuses interventions toward growth at each of the three dimensions (Lantz, 2001, 2002).

BEING "OF" THE WORLD

The phrase "being of the world" refers to the fact that the human being has a body and must obey the rules of the biological and physical world. Frankl (1969) describes this dimension as the *must* dimension of existence. At the must dimension of existence, human beings must consume food and water or they will die, must die of hypothermia if they are deprived of clothing and shelter in cold weather, and must experience depression if certain biochemical imbalances exist within the central nervous system (Lantz, 2001). In short-term existential intervention, it is important to realize that at times the client is in need of medical-oriented services, and that comprehensive intervention includes the practitioner's willingness to link the client to a medical provider when such services are needed. (See "biological coping", in chapter 2.) Common problems that originate at the must dimension of existence include cancer, heart disease, emphysema, arthritis, acute lateral sclerosis (ALS), AIDS, some forms of depression, and organic brain diseases.

The central treatment issue at the must dimension of existence is *physical vitality* (Frankl, 1969; Lantz, 1978).

BEING "IN" THE WORLD

The phrase "being in the world" refers to the fact that people have some freedoms in their existence and can make many choices in life reactive to difficulties and opportunities (Berg & Dolan, 2001; Frankl, 1955). Being "in" the world refers to the fact that all people can have an impact on their inner and outer environments and are both reactive and proactive living beings. Frankl (1997) describes this dimension of existence as the *can* dimension. In the can dimension, the person is understood as having the gifts of "intentionality" and "freedom," which can be used to differentially respond to the limitations and opportunities of life (Saleebey, 1992). Frankl (2000) reported that a human being can choose his or her attitude toward life and, in this way, manifest response-ability, or the ability to respond differentially to life and its challenges. People from different cultures may view these choices quite differently. Common problems originating in the can dimension of existence include adjustment disorders and some personality disorders (Frankl, 1975; Lantz, 1978).

The two central treatment issues at the can dimension of existence are *freedom* and *responsibility* (Frankl, 1967; Lantz, 1993).

BEING "FOR" THE WORLD

The phrase "being for the world" refers to the human responsibility to manifest a self-transcendent style of living in which people answer the call of life by taking care of other human beings, the community, and the environment (Frankl, 1978). This is the *ought* dimension. By using the term *ought,* Frankl (1975) is emphasizing that people should listen to the call of life to discover what they ought to do in order to discover a sense of meaning and purpose in life. When the sense of meaning and purpose in life is frustrated, disrupted, or ignored, the person will develop an existential vacuum that will become filled with either a developing sense of meaning and purpose or with symptoms such as depression, anxiety, or substance abuse (Frankl, 1975; Lantz, 2000).

The two central treatment issues in the ought dimension of existence are *meaning and self-transcendence* (Frankl, 1969; Lantz, 2001).

In short-term existential intervention the treatment process is used to challenge the client's methods of defense that serve to cover emotional pain (Lantz & Gregoire, 2003). The interventions, including holding, telling, mastering, and honoring, are detailed later in this chapter.

MEANING AND PURPOSE IN LIFE

What follows is a description of existential process, or the means by which all people develop a sense of meaning and purpose in their lives, based on the work of Frankl (1988).

Existentialism may be understood as one's search for, and adherence to, meanings, purposes, and commitments that reflect values lying outside the self. This approach to life may not always be appropriate to address during clinical intervention, especially when the client is absorbed in an immediate concern. It may be appropriate to address, however, when the client shows inclinations to look beyond the self and the immediate situation in dealing with an important life concern.

The ultimate life concerns include death, the experience or fear of isolation, the burdens that accompany freedom and responsibility, and life meaning and purpose. With regard to the last of these, categories of meaning may be social (making contributions to the lives of others), religious (seeking connection with spiritual objects), creative (anything that involves a unique contribution to the world outside the self), or experiential (such as the enjoyment of art, music, or literature). People aspire by their fundamental nature to engage in activities in any of these realms.

There are, however, certain emotions that may be prominent when the person does not feel satisfied. They are:

◆ Anxiety, which may be the result of uncertain threats to who a person is, his or her future well-being, and life and death, and is powered by the struggle to maintain connections with others, which are often threatened by the fragile nature of life

◆ Guilt, which may be a result of thoughts or actions that are violations of a person's code of conduct and is a sign of an internalized moral flaw

◆ Shame, which reflects one's failure to live up to a personal ideal

When these emotions are prominent in a client, they signal the possibility of an existential crisis.

The challenge for crisis practitioners is to understand their own existential inclinations and spirituality and how it affects their work. They should encourage client disclosure of existential concerns when appropriate, consider client functioning within a context of meaning (bring consistency to the client's present and ultimate concerns), and help clients identify meanings and purposes that can guide them in making growth-enhancing decisions.

In Frankl's practice of logotherapy, the *will to meaning* is a basic, enduring tendency to obtain what satisfies one's nature. The will to meaning assumes that all people have an innate drive to either create or discover meaning and purpose in life. Thus, people aspire by nature to make commitments to values beyond their mere existence and survival, although there are no specific meanings to which one should aspire. It is realized through one's passions and interests.

There are inherent problems in maintaining a will to meaning. First, having a purpose beyond the self involves an awareness of vulnerability and responsibility and a potential for tragedy, anxiety, and loss. Second, suppression of the will can result from actual experiences of guilt, suffering, and death. Frankl spoke of an "existential unconscious," with which meaning potentials are avoided in order to allow one to escape the accompanying sense of vulnerability and responsibility. This is similar to the concept of suppression in psychodynamic theory. In logotherapy, a person's awareness of an ultimate concern may lead to anxiety, so that awareness may be suppressed in an effort to be relieved of the anxiety.

General intervention perspectives in short-term intervention relative to existential crises include engaging the client more fully in life activity, encouraging the client to look externally, encouraging the client to care about something outside the self, and removing obstacles to the client's external focus (figure 3.1).

A number of instruments have been developed to assess one's purpose in life, including the Purpose in Life (PIL) test (Crumbaugh, 1968; Crumbaugh & Henrion, 1988; Crumbaugh & Maholick, 1964). This instrument was designed to operationalize Victor Frankl's ideas for measuring a person's experience of meaning and purpose. The PIL is a twenty-item scale that has been shown to have good reliability in

Figure 3.1. The intervention process.

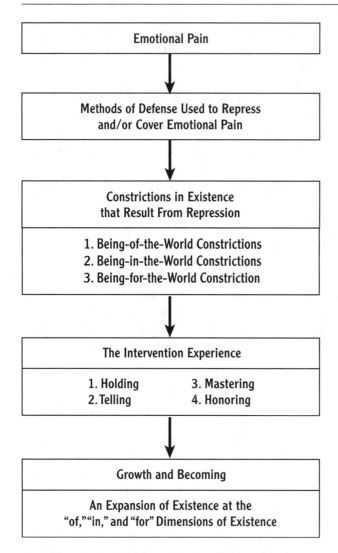

Emotional Pain

Methods of Defense Used to Repress
and/or Cover Emotional Pain

Constrictions in Existence
that Result From Repression

1. Being-of-the-World Constrictions
2. Being-in-the-World Constrictions
3. Being-for-the-World Constriction

The Intervention Experience

1. Holding   3. Mastering
2. Telling   4. Honoring

Growth and Becoming

An Expansion of Existence at the
"of," "in," and "for" Dimensions of Existence

Crumbaugh's work (0.91) and to demonstrate convergent and discriminant validity (Seeman, 1991). Each item is rated on a seven-point scale, with total scores range from 20 (low purpose) to 140 (high purpose). Examples of the twenty items include:

- ◆ I am usually: completely bored (1)—exuberant, enthusiastic (7)
- ◆ If I could choose, I would: prefer never to have been born (1)—like nine more lives just like this one (7)

- As I view the world in relation to my life, the world: completely confuses me (1)—fits meaningfully with my life (7)
- With regard to suicide, I have: thought of it seriously as a way out (1)—never given it a second thought (7) (Crumbaugh & Maholick, 1964)

A score below 93 indicates a serious disruption in the client's awareness of purpose and meaning in life. A score between 93 and 111 suggests that the person is in some danger of experiencing an existential-meaning vacuum, and a score above 112 indicates that the person is experiencing a sense of meaning and purpose.

The PIL is one means of assessing a client's sense of meaning and purpose; it is not a necessary part of the assessment. This scale should be used sparingly and should be reserved for situations in which it seems that a client would benefit from concrete evidence of his or her meaning status.

EMOTIONAL PROBLEMS AND THE THREE DIMENSIONS OF BEING

In short-term existential intervention, a crisis can be understood as any condition or occurrence that disrupts the manifestation of a client's existence on any or all three of the dimensions of existence (Lantz, 2000, 2001).

Emotional pain is defined simply as a person's negative cognitive and affective reactions to a serious problem or crisis (Grove & Haley, 1993). Such pain is often not well tolerated unless the person is fortunate enough to have access to supportive and empathic friends and family. When the emotional pain is overwhelming, or the person in crisis lacks sufficient emotional support, the person will use methods of emotional defense to cover, repress, or deny the significance of the problem (Frankl, 1969; Lantz, 2000).

A number of existential practitioners (Frankl, 1969; Lantz, 1978, Yalom, 1980) have described three primary methods of defense that are used to repress emotional pain:

1. Some people transform normal assertiveness into problematic patterns of aggression to *move against* situations and individuals that remind them of their problem experiences and pain.
2. Some people transform normal independence into problematic patterns of avoidance to *move away from* situations and individuals that remind them of their pain.
3. Some people transform normal intimacy patterns into patterns of dependence to *move toward* others in a way that gets those other people to take responsibility for overcoming their problems.

These three defense patterns can effectively cover emotional pain, but they also disrupt the person's ability to master and transform the pain into new and healthier manifestations of existence. In other words, each method of defense protects the person but also disrupts his or her ability to constructively manifest existence at the being of, being in, and being for dimensions (Lantz, 1978, 2000, 2001).

PRINCIPLES OF INTERVENTION: HOLDING, TELLING, MASTERING, AND HONORING

Working with clients is an artistic process that blends human and technical elements. Although it is important for the existential practitioner to have a well-developed knowledge base and treatment framework, the specific nature of that work is always unique to the interactive characteristics of client and practitioner. The practitioner and client freshly re-create the unique nature of intervention during their interactions (Lantz & Gregoire, 2000a; Lee & Greene, 1999). Viktor Frankl (1969) made this point in a famous treatment formula, T = X + Y, where T = good therapy, X = the unique treatment needs of the client, and Y = the unique characteristics and capacities of the therapist. Although such creativity is a hallmark of existential intervention, an artistic healing process occurs most frequently when the practitioner helps the client to hold the pain, tell the pain, master the pain, and honor the pain (Lantz, 1993, 2002). The following sections of this chapter will describe and illustrate this art.

Holding the Pain

People often ignore, avoid, deny, cover, or push significant interpersonal problems into the unconscious level of awareness in order to avoid the experience of pain (Lantz, 1993). In existential intervention, *holding* refers to a process of holding up the problem experience so it may be seen, remembered, and reexperienced by the client. Unfortunately, holding up the painful experience involves reexperiencing the pain and suffering that is at the core of the problem (Lantz, 1993). Holding up the pain can also include catharsis. As a client remembers, holds up, and reexperiences the negative feelings, there is often a release of pain that reduces (but does not eliminate) the client's ongoing suffering.

Sometimes holding is described as empathic availability (Marcel, 1948). Empathic availability is a committed presence to the "other" and openness to the pain and potentials of the other even when such openness is difficult and unpleasant (Lantz, 2000). When manifesting empathic availability, the existential practitioner does not hide from the client's pain behind a stance of objectivity or abstraction, nor behind a belief in a rigid interpretation of his or her role. Although the practitioner must remember to persist with a well-formulated intervention stance, such a concern should not result in blunted compassion, or a distancing of the practitioner from the client's pain. Empathic availability often provides the client with the support he or she needs to tell the story of his or her problem experiences. Empathic availability gives the client a feeling of being understood (Lantz, 2001).

The risks of empathic availability are that the practitioner may begin to experi-

Figure 3.2. Results in an adequate holding environment and epathetic availability.

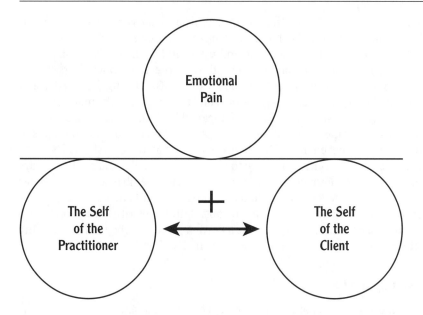

ence secondary stress disorder symptoms. That is, when a practitioner is helping the client hold up the intense pain, the practitioner will begin to experience bits of the client's pain (Coady, 1993; Lantz, 1993). This process is illustrated in figure 3.2. The existential practitioner's empathic availability and willingness to help hold and share the client's pain allows the client to remember or openly reexperience that pain without defensiveness. The client is often able to reexperience emotional pain in proportion to the practitioner's empathic availability. In the absence of such empathy, the client will continue to repress the awareness of emotional pain (Lantz, 2000).

Telling the Pain

Telling, talking about, and naming emotional pain is the second element of existential intervention (Lantz, 1993; Lee, Sebold, & Uken, 2003). Paradoxically, *telling* the pain both depends on the development of empathic availability between the practitioner and client and powerfully facilitates the development of such an encounter. Telling the pain is helpful to the client for two reasons. First, such telling places the emotional experience and pain into the world of mutual encounter, where the relationship between client and practitioner can be used to process the situation under circumstances of increased support (Lantz, 1978; Lee, Sebold, & Uken, 2003). Telling emotional experience brings pain out of the internal world of the client and into the interactional world of mutual awareness, understanding, and support (Bell, 1995; Lantz, 1978).

A second reason why telling the pain is helpful has to do with the power of naming. When a client can describe, tell, and name the emotions he or she has experienced, this often begins the processing and mastering of the crisis (Lantz, 2002; Turner, 1996). Telling and naming occurred during intervention with Mrs. Jones. Mrs. Jones was an adult survivor of childhood sexual abuse. During the fourth treatment session, the client was able to remember and tell about how the man next door had forced her to perform oral sex (i.e., oral rape) on him while she was a child. She also was able to remember and tell how this man would take nude photographs of her before and after the oral rape. Mrs. Jones reported that for years she had become horribly nervous whenever anyone tried to photograph her. She said she had always felt "nuts" about this photophobia until she was able to remember and tell about her awful childhood experiences. Telling and renaming the events that caused her photophobia helped Mrs. Jones to feel more in control. In her words, she no longer felt like a "mental case." Instead, she felt "like a normal person—who the hell wouldn't have gotten afraid if this kind of stuff had happened to them?"

Mastering the Pain

Mastering the emotional pain is a process of reflection and behavioral experimentation that helps a client discover unique healing activities that are useful in processing and defusing the problem situation (Brunson, 2002; Corcoran, 2001). From an existential point of view, helping a client to transform aggression into assertiveness, avoidance into independence, and dependency into the ability to experience intimacy is a powerful way for him or her to master emotional experiences (Lantz, 1978). Mastering the pain helps a client develop freedom at the being of the world dimension of existence (Frankl, 1959). For Viktor Frankl (1969) mastering a crisis includes noticing and actualizing a meaning potential that is hidden in the crisis experience or, in other words, taking advantage of a growth opportunity.

Honoring the Pain

Honoring the pain refers to the process of celebrating the meaning potentials and opportunities in the problem situation that the client actualizes and makes real. To Viktor Frankl (1959), honoring emotional pain involves becoming consciously aware of some of the opportunities for self-transcendent giving to the world that are embedded in the problem situation and the client's memory. During the process of honoring the pain, the practitioner helps the client to find and actualize a desire to give birth to another's joy or facilitate the cessation of another's pain, which occurs as a result of his or her empathic understanding of the pain of other human beings (Lantz, 2000, 2001). This helps the client to manifest existence at the being for the world dimension. Honoring is a celebration of the mastering of one's emotional pain.

Honoring the pain associated with an emotional problem has been described by Viktor Frankl (1959, 1969) as a way to "fill the existential-meaning vacuum" that often occurs reactive to a traumatic experience. He asserts that only the manifestation of human love can overcome the negative effects of such experiences. Honoring the pain occurs through the manifestation of human availability in the face of emotional pain. Honoring the experience is both an outgrowth of mastery and a facilitating factor in the development of a client's sense of mastery and control (Lantz, 1978, 1993, 1998).

The following examples illustrate the short-term existential intervention process of holding, telling, mastering, and honoring the client's experiences and pain.

SANDY JAMES

Mr. and Mrs. James requested mental health services for their eighteen-year-old daughter, who was depressed and "wants to die." Sandy's depression had started immediately after she survived an auto accident in which three of her friends died on the day preceding their senior prom and two weeks before their graduation from high school. Sandy and her friends had been drinking. Although Sandy had not been driving, she felt guilty that she was alive while her friends had died. Sandy was no longer motivated to go to college, wanted to stay at home all day long, could not sleep, could not eat much food, had lost ten pounds, and manifested frequent crying spells. Sandy had a good preaccident history of social functioning, and her problems seemed directly related to her crisis experience of the accident. Sandy's parents asked the practitioner to "fix our child."

Sandy and her parents were seen together in existential intervention on five occasions. The focus of the intervention was to facilitate the family's ability to hold, tell, master, and honor their emotional pain. The central issue in working with the James family was to help the parents discover that they could deal with their own and Sandy's pain as a family and did not need to turn their daughter over to an "expert stranger." Sandy went on to college, getting good grades, and becoming an active volunteer with a national anti-substance organization. She was a frequent speaker at high schools, telling about what happened to her three best friends after drinking and driving. In those ways Sandy was able to tell, master, and honor her crisis pain.

MRS. BROWN

Mr. and Mrs. Brown were referred for intervention after Mrs. Brown had trouble "bouncing back emotionally" after breast surgery for cancer and, later, chemotherapy. Mrs. Brown experienced crying spells, weight loss, energy loss, and anxiety attacks when she went out in public. She attempted to use antidepressant medications but stopped taking them because of side effects that she did not wish to tolerate. The Browns were referred for intervention by their oncologist after Mrs. Brown reported that she wanted help for herself and her husband in learning how to face not having a breast. Both Mr. and Mrs. Brown also complained that the breast surgery and chemotherapy had disrupted their sex life.

The Browns were seen for intervention on four occasions. The couple was helped to express their emotional pain (holding), talk openly to each other about their pain (telling), work out some of their sexual difficulties that were reactive to the crisis of losing a breast and facing cancer (mastering), and, finally, to find some way of helping others who face cancer in honor of their own experience (honoring). Mr. and Mrs. Brown became active in fundraising efforts for the American Cancer Society and reported a good adjustment at a one-year follow-up evaluation.

SUMMARY

Existentialism can be understood as one's search for, and adherence to, meanings, purposes, and commitments that lie beyond the self. Short-term existential intervention is based on the humanistic concepts of Viktor Frankl and the family treatment concepts developed by Jim Lantz and his colleagues. In Frankl's logotherapy, the will to meaning is a basic, enduring tendency to obtain what satisfies one's nature. This will assumes that all people have an innate drive to either create or discover meaning and purpose in life.

In short-term existential intervention, it is the practitioner's responsibility to help clients resolve their problems and challenges in the context of ultimate life meanings through the process of holding, telling, mastering, and honoring pain. Short-term existential intervention has shown to be effective in a variety of crisis situations and in both public agency and private practice settings. The approach has been useful with Vietnam veterans living with the symptoms of PTSD, clients facing the crisis of migration and the death of a beloved family member, clients facing life stage change, and clients attempting to overcome the trauma of physical abuse or rape.

4

Emotional Motivation for Short-Term Existential Intervention

DIAGNOSIS IN CRISIS INTERVENTION (OR ANY TYPE OF CLINICAL PRACTICE) is a complicated affair. Attempts have been made to utilize symptom manifestation as a basis for diagnosis (Turner, 2002), and problem-centered typologies have also been developed (Cowger & Snively, 2002; DeJong, 2002; Haley, 1976). Although all such efforts are useful, each assessment system is limited in scope. Existential practitioners must utilize multiple assessment systems, and the practitioner's subjective impressions will always be an important part of the clinical assessment (Lantz, 1978; Saulnier, 2001).

This chapter discusses the critical assessment issue of the client's emotional motivation to engage in changing his or her thoughts, feelings, and behaviors. There are a number of motivation assessments available; one will be presented briefly, and another, less well known but more useful for existential intervention, will be presented in some detail.

First, the Transtheoretical Stages of Change (TSOC) model is a recent formulation of how practitioners may understand the conflicting thoughts and feelings that underlie a client's degree of motivation to change (DiClemente & Prochaska, 1998). Developed first in the substance abuse field, it asserts that ambivalence characterizes many, if not most, significant change situations, and that clients pass through a series of steps as they resolve their ambivalence and approach the point of change. These stages are *precontemplation, contemplation, preparation, action, maintenance,* and *problem relapse.* Understanding the steps involved in a change process can be helpful for all crisis practitioners, as it helps them appreciate how clients struggle with even recognizing a need for change. Practitioners can then help clients to face and resolve the ambivalence that accompanies many change opportunities.

While the TSOC is a useful model for practitioners, the model presented here looks more uniquely at each client's way of *feeling* the change process. This tool grows out of the original motivational work of Sandor Rado (1942) and uses the client's most prominent emotional motivation for treatment as the basis for both assessment and intervention. The four kinds of clients described in this framework are the magical-craving, parental-invocation, cooperative-striving, and realistic self-reliant types (Lantz, 1978; Rado, 1942).

EMOTIONAL MOTIVATION FOR TREATMENT

Rado's (1942) motivational framework is designed to categorize the client's emotional expectations about how the client and practitioner should go about determining the goals of intervention, and how the intervention process should unfold. Like other categorization tools, this one is not perfect; and no client can be perfectly described by the framework. Each client manifests, to some degree, all the motivational forms, although one is usually most prominent. Once the client's primary emotional motivation for treatment is identified, the practitioner can utilize intervention techniques that support appropriate curative factors, or strategies to achieve crisis resolution and growth, that correspond with that level (see table 4.1).

Each motivational stance includes both problematic and adaptational (or strengths) qualities. For example, a client who is motivated to have a practitioner take care of him or her (parental invocation) is manifesting a type of problem, insofar as the client may approach all relationships from a dependent position. At the same time, this motivation is also adaptive. It may well represent the client's best form of social functioning, and it is probably effective at times. Thus, asking clients to change their emotional motivation for intervention early in the process is like asking the client to no longer need intervention! If the existential practitioner can understand and accept the adaptational qualities of the client's motivation, he or she

Table 4.1. Emotional motivations for intervention

Motivational Level	Curative Factor	Intervention Techniques
Magical craving	Prestige suggestion	Indirect suggestion, charismatic permission, symbolic structure, and/or ritual
Parental invocation	Support	Empathy, ventilation acceptance, encouragement, environmental modification
Cooperative striving	Experiential validation	Confrontation and reality testing, pattern clarification, social skills training, cognitive restructuring, behavior modification
Realistic self-reliant	Insight (developmental and/or existential)	Interpretation, encounter, Socratic search for meaning

can join with the client in a beginning treatment alliance. The possibility of the client's initial reactance is minimized, and the opportunity to help the client develop a more balanced form of emotional motivation is not as likely to be lost to a premature termination.

One implication of assessing a client's emotional motivation for treatment is that he or she can be matched with practitioners who have particular skills with any of the four types of motivation. We will consider this point in more detail later in the chapter.

The Magical-Craving Client

The *magical-craving* client wants a miracle to happen that will resolve his or her problems, and the client thus projects magical powers onto the practitioner. The client then feels better, not because the practitioner has done anything helpful, but because the client believes that the practitioner can and will perform magic through the ritual of regular intervention sessions (Lantz, 1978; Rado, 1942). On an emotional level, magical-craving clients do not understand the process of cause and effect. These clients frequently have thought disorders, such as those found in clients with psychosis, extreme mood problems, and personality disorders. Such clients engage in magical thinking, exhibit ideas of reference, and often experience delusions and hallucinations. In many crisis situations, of course, clients frequently experience massive levels of anxiety, and at those times any client can regress to this motivational level.

Prestige suggestion is the curative factor that is initially most helpful to the magical-craving client. Instead of confronting the client's expectations, the practitioner initially accepts the client's motivational stance. The practitioner does not try to perform magic or say that he or she can perform magic. The practitioner makes helpful suggestions and allows the client's magical expectations of success to trigger improvement (Frank & Frank, 1993). Prestige suggestion is facilitated by the use of suggestion, charismatic permission, and symbolic structure or ritual (Lantz, 1978; Rado, 1942). The following case example illustrates this curative factor.

THE SHAFER FAMILY

The Shafers were an urban Appalachian family that requested mental health services after their twenty-three-year-old son was released from a state psychiatric hospital. The son had nine psychiatric admissions in six years. He had consistently been diagnosed as suffering from paranoid schizophrenia, and he manifested auditory hallucinations, ideas of reference, paranoid thinking, loose associations, and ambivalence about all significant life issues. The family described themselves as being in chaos as they adjusted to the son's return from the hospital with active symptoms of psychosis.

The social history information revealed that Mrs. Shafer had herself experienced four psychiatric hospital admissions in the past. She reported problems with impulse control, suicidal thinking, anxiety attacks, and derealization experiences. She stated that she had been diagnosed as "a borderline" and that she always dropped out of treatment "when I got feeling better." Mr. Shafer reported that he was addicted to alcohol. He stated, "I do good when I go to AA." He also reported that "I drink to get rid of the voices" and that at times the voices "tell me that I don't deserve the help I get at AA." Mr. and Mrs. Shafer reported, "God doesn't answer our prayers." Mrs. Shafer and the son were both receiving Social Security disability funds, and Mr. Shafer was not working at the time because of his alcoholism. Mrs. Shafer reported that her son always dropped out of treatment because she would "get nervous" and would not take him to his appointments. She stated that she sometimes got the feeling that she "shouldn't leave home or something bad will happen."

This challenging family did extremely well in treatment. They were able to accept medication, social advocacy, and environmental support because they believed that the practitioner was "more powerful than the voices." The practitioner utilized concrete instructions and specific suggestions to help the family members develop more structure in their daily lives. He also gave the family a schedule of family activities related to social and home maintenance functions for them to perform. Mr. and Mrs. Shafer reported that the schedule was "magic" and that they could "chase the voices away" by looking at the family schedule. The practitioner's initial use of structure and the ritual of frequent appointments were successful because of the family's magical-craving stance.

The Parental-Invocation Client

Parental invocation is similar to the developmental stage in which the child strongly relies upon the parents. The adaptational level of the client is still primitive in that most parental-invocation clients believe that they must rely upon a stronger and more powerful significant other. The client attempts to get the practitioner to do everything for him or her and expects problems to be solved through the practitioner's efforts rather than his or her own efforts (Rado, 1942). The parental-invocation client is able to use cause-and-effect thinking in understanding situations but does not believe that he or she has the power to influence a personal psychosocial situation. Such clients generally are depressed. Again, under extreme stress, any client can regress to this motivational level (Lantz, 1978; Rado, 1942).

Support is the curative factor that is most helpful to the parental-invocation client. The practitioner does not initially reject the giving role and does not challenge the client to take responsibility for the self. The client is supported through the use of empathy, ventilation acceptance, encouragement, and environmental manipulation. The following case illustrates the use of support with a parental-invocation client.

MR. THOMAS

Mr. Thomas was an African American man who requested treatment shortly after his father died and his wife ran off with another man. He reported that he worked full time, had two kids to care for, and felt depressed and overwhelmed. He reported suicidal thinking, energy loss, crying spells, and confused thinking. He reported that his nine-year-old son had started wetting the bed and that his seven-year-old daughter was afraid to go to school. The practitioner arranged for Mr. Thomas to see a psychiatrist, who placed him on antidepressant medication, and called a child-welfare agency to help Mr. Thomas obtain homemaker and child-care services. Both Mr. Thomas and his two children were seen twice weekly so that they could express their feelings about the recent loss of their wife and mother. The practitioner's attitude was supportive, and concrete environmental services were also arranged.

Mr. Thomas made excellent progress. Within one month both he and the children showed concrete evidence of considerable relief from their symptoms of depression. The father reported that "When I was really down, you helped by giving support.". He also stated that it helped when the practitioner "took over" and made arrangements that "I couldn't do myself." Both emotional support and concrete environmental services were indicated because the client was overwhelmed and needed "someone else to do something." Under stress, the father had regressed to the parental-invocation level of motivation, and as the issues were resolved he was able to work at a higher motivational level.

The Cooperative-Striving Client

In the motivational level of *cooperative-striving* clients do not want the practitioner to do anything for them, but they want the practitioner to tell them what to do. The client requests direction, advice, guidance, and suggestions. These clients feel strong enough to do problem resolution work but do not feel adequate to determine the work that they should do. The cooperative-striving level of motivation may be comparable to the stage of adolescence in human development. The client hopes to retain autonomy of action but does not feel comfortable with either goal setting or the identification of effective solutions or problem-solving activities (Lantz, 1978; Rado, 1942). Many clients who request marital therapy demonstrate this type of treatment motivation. They do not want the practitioner to run their lives, but they do expect the professional to provide adequate direction and guidance.

Experiential validation is the intervention stance that is most helpful to the cooperative-striving client. This is a process of interactional or problem-solving experimentation in which the client learns emotionally what adaptive solutions work and feel best. The practitioner works with the client to reflect on and consider a variety of change strategies that the client might attempt with the support of the practitioner. Such intervention techniques include confrontation and reality testing, pattern clarification, social-skills training, cognitive restructuring, and behavior modification. The following case illustrates the use of experiential validation with a cooperative-striving couple.

THE LEE FAMILY

Mr. and Mrs. Lee were a Korean American couple who requested marital therapy after their youngest child left home to go to college. They were experiencing considerable domestic conflict and wanted to improve their communication with each other. Mrs. Lee stated that she was shy and that she got very anxious when she talked about problems or feelings. Mr. Lee stated that he had never been comfortable with conflict and that he tended to avoid it whenever possible. Both of them wanted the practitioner to suggest ways that they could talk with each other about feelings, conflicts, and problems. They expressed a willingness to do whatever the practitioner said, since he was "an expert." The practitioner told them that they should join a marital couples group and use the weekly group sessions as a practice laboratory in which to experiment and find ways to talk about feelings with each other. The practitioner advised them that he, the cotherapist, and the other group members would suggest ways to communicate, but that it would be up to Mr. and Mrs. Lee to try them out in lab and to see how they felt. The couple was eager to join the group, with the practitioner's endorsement, and they made good use of the intervention and their practices.

The Realistic Self-Reliant Client

The *realistic self-reliant* client is not interested in magic, concrete help, or advice from the practitioner. The client wants to figure things out for him or herself. These clients use intervention to discover how to make full use of their own potential. They are often described as growth-oriented clients. Their motivational level corresponds with that of adulthood. Such clients are interested in both insight and encounter.

Insight is the curative factor that is most helpful to the realistic self-reliant client. Insight can be developmental (related to age-appropriate behaviors), pattern-specific (related to habitual ways of thinking, feeling, and behaving), or existential (related to meaning in life issues). Intervention techniques that stimulate this curative factor include transference interpretations; encounter experiences during the intervention sessions, and the Socratic search (through reflective questioning) for meaning. The following case illustrates how insight can be used with a realistic self-reliant family. This example also describes an interesting countertransference issue.

THE CARTER FAMILY

The Carters were an Italian American family who requested family crisis intervention because their fourteen-year-old son had attempted to run away from home several times. The family members wanted to understand why he ran away and how they could improve the situation. They were feeling increasingly unsettled in this situation, and household tensions had become high. The son's pattern of running away had started a few months after the father was diagnosed with leukemia. The parents stated that they did not believe it was necessary to spend time talking about the leukemia because medical authorities were handling the disease. They felt that family therapy was only necessary to help them figure out how to help their son stop running away.

Despite the obvious connection between the onset of the problem and the father's diagnosis of leukemia, the practitioner did not push the family to talk about the illness. The practitioner actually ran away in this situation. He avoided the subject for several sessions until a colleague asked him how he was doing with the Carter family in light of the fact that "Mr. Carter has a serious illness like your father does." The practitioner had completely denied any connection between his work with the Carter family and the fact that his own father had a serious heart condition and was undergoing surgery in the near future. In other words, the practitioner was in denial over his own family situation. He recognized the problem immediately and then decided to change his approach with the Carter family.

In the next family session, the practitioner told the family that he was having difficulty working with them. He shared his feelings (fear, anxiety, concern, and grief) about his own father's serious medical condition. He told the family that he wanted to run away from his own feelings about his father and that he felt he was helping them run away from their own feelings about Mr. Carter's condition. At this point, the son began to cry and talked about his fears. He stated that no one wanted to talk about the father's problems and that he felt all alone. The practitioner suggested to the son that perhaps the two of them should run away together. The father then shared his feelings about also wanting to run away. The mother pointed out that she felt all alone and was afraid to talk about anything. The family finally decided to "run away with one another" and talk about the leukemia while they were running away. Intervention sessions were increased to twice weekly and were conceptualized as "family run-away time." The son stopped running away physically, and the family started dealing with one another about the father's illness. All family members reported that they were now at least happy to be talking to one another in a substantive way.

SUPPORT, CONFRONTATION, AND THE MOTIVATIONAL FRAMEWORK

Existential intervention generally provides the client with the opportunity to experience all four curative factors described above. Rado's (1942) framework can help the practitioner to determine the curative factor that will initially be most supportive to the client. When the existential practitioner uses treatment techniques that stimulate a curative factor that is compatible with the client's treatment motivation, the sense of perceived support is maximized. On the other hand, when the practitioner uses intervention techniques that stimulate a curative factor that is not compatible with the client's treatment motivation, then the client experiences the approach as confrontational. Still, such confrontation may be useful in that it challenges the client to move to another level of motivation; one that is closer to self-reliance. In this way the emotional motivation framework is a useful tool for helping the practitioner balance supportive and confrontational techniques during intervention.

THE RELATIONSHIP BETWEEN EMOTIONAL MOTIVATION AND COUNTERTRANSFERENCE

The term *countertransference* was initially defined as a practitioner's unconscious reactions to the client's projections (Jacobs, 1999). This concept has broadened to refer to the effects of the practitioner's conscious and unconscious needs and wishes on his or her understanding of the client. It also refers to the conscious attitudes and tendencies that the practitioner has about types of clients (such as being drawn to working with children or having an aversion to older adults).

Countertransference during intervention is a process that can be utilized either constructively or problematically. When recognized, monitored, and appropriately managed, countertransference can aid the assessment process, the development of practitioner empathy, and effective treatment planning. Negative countertransference during intervention often occurs when the practitioner finds it difficult to tolerate the client's motivational stance or emotional pain. This was seen in the previous case, and the following case illustrates another countertransference problem experienced by a practitioner.

ONE UP, ONE DOWN

In my first job as a therapist, I worked with children and parents with severe behavioral and emotional problems. I had excellent results with this population using family-treatment and crisis intervention forms of therapy. I worked with clients who had schizophrenia and their families in my second job. Again, my results were positive. My third job, however, was at a counseling center in the suburbs of a large city. In this position, I did not work with severely disturbed clients, but with more motivated, growth-oriented families. I provided process-oriented, experiential family-treatment services. The results were terrible!

My lack of effectiveness caused me considerable personal distress. With the advice of a supportive supervisor, I joined a therapy group. The material that emerged during therapy centered on my internal comfort whenever I was in either a one-up (controlling) or a one-down (subservient) interpersonal situation, and the internal discomfort that I experienced whenever I was in a more equal interpersonal situation. It was revealed that during my first few years of professional practice, I worked with magical-craving and parental-invocation clients—a population that did not challenge my interpersonal style. In the third job, however, I worked primarily with cooperative-striving and realistic self-reliant clients who required a more democratic intervention relationship. These clients challenged my interpersonal style. My own therapy experience helped me identify and work through many of these problems.

The emotional-motivation framework can help the practitioner to predict which clients will tend to stimulate residual negative countertransference feelings. My work with cooperative-striving and realistic self-reliant families has improved. I have also found that the motivational framework helps practitioners whom I supervise identify and manage their countertransference problems.

MATCHING PRACTITIONERS AND CLIENTS

The vignette above brings to mind the potential for matching clients and practitioners based on the types of emotional motivation with which they are most attuned and effective. There have been efforts made to match clinical practitioners and clients on certain variables (such as race, age, gender, ethnicity), but these have produced mixed results thus far. With regard to the TSOC model described earlier in this chapter, it has been found that practitioners who focus on the client's appropriate stage of change have greater success than those practitioners who do not assess that variable (Miller & Rollnick, 2002). Aside from the TSOC studies, however, no other research has been done on matching clients by motivational characteristics. Although research in this area is minimal, it seems that existential practitioners and supervisors may benefit from using this variable in their client assessment work and practitioner evaluations.

SUMMARY

In this chapter, Rado's model of emotional motivation dynamics, featuring the categories of magical craving, parental invocation, cooperative striving, and realistic self-reliance, was outlined, and its use with clients described. The importance of the practitioner matching his or her interventions to the client's primary type of emotional motivation was illustrated through case material. The chapter also explained how the practitioner's own levels of comfort or discomfort with clients may be dependent in some ways on the clients' level of emotional motivation. That is, the practitioner may be more suited to addressing certain client orientations, although with awareness and perhaps some assistance this comfort and capacity level may be broadened.

5

Vicious Circles in Short-Term Existential Intervention

MUCH OF THE LITERATURE ON SHORT-TERM CLINICAL INTERVENTION IN-dicates that a variety of approaches have a positive influence on clients' recovery and enhanced functioning (See Corwin, 2002, for a review). Because of these positive outcomes across intervention models, it is possible that there are common themes addressed by practitioners from a variety of orientations that, if identified, might provide a framework for general practical guidelines. One example is a set of common themes that has been articulated by Frank and Frank (1992), who engaged in a cross-cultural survey of the characteristics of professional helpers. They concluded that common factors among intervention approaches that seem to predict effectiveness include:

◆ The development of an emotionally charged, confiding relationship between the worker and client in which the practitioner provides the client with a sense of his or her competence and caring as well as an antidote to alienation, enhanced morale, and the determination to persist with problem resolution
◆ A setting that creates the expectation of help (featuring the elements of client safety and support for the worker's perceived prestige)
◆ An optimistic view of human nature that is compatible with the client's worldview, helps the client make sense of his or her problems, requires active participation from the worker and client, and helps the client perceive shortcomings and corrective possibilities

Another example of client features that are found in many emotional problem presentations is what is often called the *vicious circle* of problem behavior (Hoffman, 1976; Wender, 1968). Attention to this phenomenon may be useful toward developing a general unifying intervention framework. While attention to this intra- or interpersonal feature is useful for existential practitioners, it may also useful to those practicing from different orientations.

The vicious circle may be understood as a pattern of behaviors, usually within an interpersonal system, that has become a habitual means of responding to problems and challenges. It represents an automatic rather than a proactive response to a presenting problem, and as such it is not always an effective means of resolving problems. The patterns demonstrated by one member of the interpersonal system in turn evoke habitual response patterns from other members in the system. People often fall into these circular habits of problem-solving behavior, erroneously assuming that what has been effective in the past will be effective in the future. The vicious circle is considered to be a central concept in many forms of short-term intervention, and the concept is also highly regarded in strategic and solution-focused intervention approaches (Nichols & Schwartz, 2005).

INDIVIDUAL, DYAD, AND TRIAD VICIOUS CIRCLES

The vicious circle may occur in the context of an individual, dyad, or triadic system (Lantz, 1978). An example of the *individual* form of the vicious circle is an athlete who, because of age or accumulating physical stress, is beginning to lose some of his or her speed and coordination. The circular sequence unfolds as follows:

1. The athlete's physical abilities begin to decline with age or stress.
2. The athlete evaluates the decrease in ability as a serious threat to his or her identity.
3. The athlete avoids competition to insulate him or herself against the pain of the negative self-evaluation.
4. The athlete experiences further decrease in performance ability by avoiding competition.
5. The athlete experiences a greater threat to identity.
6. The athlete increasingly avoids competition.

A common example of the *dyadic* vicious circle may occur between an aggressive wife and a passive husband, illustrated by the following sequence of events:

1. The husband experiences anxiety associated with contact with his aggressive, critical wife.
2. The husband avoids this anxiety by withdrawing from the wife.
3. The wife feels left out of the relationship.
4. The wife shouts at her husband in an attempt to make more contact.
5. The husband increases his avoidance behavior in response to the shouting.
6. The wife feels even more alone and increases her shouting in another attempt to make contact.

A common form of a *triadic* cycle operates as follows:

1. An adolescent son becomes argumentative with his mother.
2. The mother complains to her husband rather than talking to the son.
3 The husband, who is not directly involved with the mother/son issue, scolds the son in a half-hearted way.

4. The son argues with his mother again.
5. The mother complains to her husband.
6. The husband tells his wife that she can't handle her son.
7. The son continues to provoke arguments with his mother.
8. The wife complains to her husband yet again.
9. The husband becomes more convinced that his wife is the problem.

The specific nature of each form of the vicious circle has implications for intervention, as discussed later in this chapter.

TWO CLASSES OF THE VICIOUS CIRCLE

There are two major classes of the vicious circle, and each can occur in an individual, dyad, or triad situation. Furthermore, both forms can be in operation at the same time in the same situation, and in those cases they may perpetuate each other.

The first class can be called the *deviation-amplifying* or *snowball* form of the vicious circle. This concept was originally identified by Marujama (1963) and was further elaborated by Wender (1968). This form of vicious circle is similar to a snowball rolling down a hill, gaining strength and momentum along the way. As the snowball moves it picks up weight, which then causes it to move faster. The earlier example of the athlete represents a form of the snowball vicious circle: the person's behavior cycle led to a problem continuing to grow until it reached a crisis point. In that example, the athlete's decreased performance was evaluated as a threat to identify and led to an avoidance of competition, which amplified the deviation in performance. This amplified the negative evaluation and the threat to identify. The net effect is a circular process that escalates over time until professional intervention may be necessary to reverse the process.

A second form of vicious circle is the *homeostatic* cycle (Hoffman, 1976). This cycle functions in such a way that a symptom develops in one member of a system for the purpose of disguising or minimizing problem behaviors in other members of the system. This process is often seen with children and their parents. A common example of this vicious circle in a triadic form is the "minor as marital therapist" syndrome (Lantz, 1993, 2000). In this process, the parents have covertly agreed not to discuss with each other any problems, conflicts, or concerns in their own relationship, as a means of maintaining homeostasis, or a steady state. As a result, both parents experience suppressed anger toward each other, although this is usually denied. From time to time their anger begins to surface, however, and at those times one of the children becomes anxious and develops symptoms of a disorder. The parental conflict is subsequently avoided as the parents work together to help the child. The child is thus reinforced for his or her symptom development (by receiving attention and assistance), and the parents' mutual avoidance is reinforced by the relief they feel about not having to deal with their own conflicts. The child's symptom thus functions to prevent parental conflict and acts as cement for the parents' marriage. The process is circular and usually continues, and it may escalate until the child develops a set of behaviors that can be given a psychiatric label. Even after such labeling has occurred, the process may continue until the professional helper can involve the parents in a process of facing and working out their marital problems.

The homeostatic circle is more difficult to interrupt than the deviation-amplifying circle. It is a more subtle manifestation of the vicious circle and may be difficult to assess, given that the practitioner often meets with the family at a slice in time.

THE SPEED OF VICIOUS CIRCLES

Not only can the two classes of the vicious circle occur in individual, dyad, and triad forms, but they also occur at different rates of speed. For example, the previously mentioned minor as marital therapist sequence can sometimes play out and be identified in its entirety during a single family therapy session. On the other hand, some vicious circles may not be completed in less than one year. The practitioner's discovery of this more gradual vicious circle sequence cannot be made without the completion of a comprehensive family history. Because vicious circles occur at different speed rates, short-term practitioners who do not rely on extensive family history or other assessment data not experiential in nature may miss important clues that could identify a vicious circle sequence (Coady, 1993; Lantz, 1978).

VICIOUS CIRCLES AMONG DIFFERENT CATEGORIES OF PEOPLE

In most instances, vicious circles occur in dyad or triad forms and develop among individuals from the same family group. At times, however, the circle will include one or more individuals from outside the family group, but still within the client's boundary of socially and emotionally significant people (such as friends, neighbors, extended family members, and coworkers). Sometimes the vicious circle will occur between the family as a group and one or more social agencies and organizations. For example, a family may become caught in a homeostatic vicious circle of interaction with a school system, in which a child member acts out a family conflict in that setting. School staff may collude with the family by labeling the child as delinquent even when that child is behaving in a way that is holding the family together.

It is important to remember that vicious circles can occur between different categories of people and institutions; otherwise the practitioner may develop overly rigid rules about the range of persons who may participate in the intervention. As a general rule it is useful to look first to the members of the natural family group as the most likely people to be involved in a problem situation that may involve a vicious circle. If the complete sequence cannot be identified when the natural family group is assessed, the practitioner should consider other individuals within the client's social and emotional network (Lantz, 1978). If a thorough screening of individuals within the family and social boundaries of the patient does not reveal the existence of a vicious circle, the practitioner may assume that the circle is individual in nature.

The following social functioning map identifies the territories in which vicious circles may occur (figure 5.1).

ASSESSMENT GUIDELINES

When an individual manifests emotional pain or develops behavior that has been labeled a psychiatric symptom, that person may be signaling the presence of a vicious circle sequence. After noting such a signal, the practitioner should attempt to determine the following:

1. The type of vicious circle in which the client is involved (Is it a deviation-amplifying or homeostatic cycle process, or a combination of the two?)
2. The persons who are participating in the vicious circle sequence (Is the circle an individual, dyad, or triad process?)

Figure 5.1. Clinical intervention territory map.

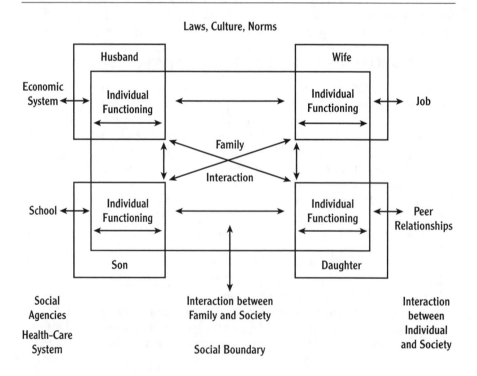

3. The speed of the vicious circle sequence (Is it slow or fast?)
4. The social territory in which the vicious circle occurs (Does it cross individual, family, or social boundaries, and what categories of people or institutions are involved?)
5. Any blocking procedures that the practitioner can use that will effectively and efficiently interrupt the vicious circle sequence, allowing more functional patterns to emerge

INTERVENTION GUIDELINES

Vicious circle interventions will depend upon the type, form, and speed of the circle, as well as the territory in which it occurs. If the vicious circle is of the deviation-amplifying form, intervention approaches can be fairly direct. For example, in the illustration where the wife shouted at the husband (who then avoided contact, which then caused the wife to escalate her shouting), a simple directive, such as having the wife avoid the husband more often, may well interrupt and change the entire process. On the other hand, when the vicious circle is of the homeostatic form, the practitioner may need to use a series of interventions to bring the avoided behavior out into the open.

For example, one way of interrupting the minor as marital therapist syndrome is for the practitioner to relabel the marital pair's efforts to help the child as evidence of differences and conflict between the husband and wife. Such relabeling places the child in the position where his or her symptom no longer prevents marital conflict and, as a result, the child's symptom may disappear. The direction of intervention can then be changed to help the marital pair work through some of their problems.

Vicious circles that include two or more participating individuals can often be handled effectively in conjoint interviews. The conjoint interview allows the vicious circle process to occur experientially in front of the practitioner, and as a result more data and opportunities for intervention will be manifested. Vicious circles that involve only one person's participation can be treated in a conjoint interview through the labeling of the circular process by the practitioner as a way the individual obtains or avoids contact with others. This changes the vicious circle into a transactional process and increases opportunities for change within the system. Group intervention may be used when the client does not have a significant other who can be involved in the helping process. The group members help each other identify and work through their problematic circular behaviors.

When a vicious circle crosses the family boundary to include individuals who are not family members, but who exist within the boundary of the patient's socially significant people or social organizations, the family-centered practitioner must frame the outsider's participation in a way that facilitates constructive interactions. Reasons for the outsider's participation should be articulated as help for the family or identified client rather than as necessary due to his or her participation in a problematic vicious circle sequence. This is because persons outside the family system, including social organization representatives, are often quite reluctant to recognize the part they may be playing in a vicious circle. Members of a school system, for example, (teachers, administrators, and even social workers) may be reluctant to see or empathize with the notion that the student's acting-out behavior is an effort to keep other members of a family system from facing their own conflicts.

When other organizations are involved in a vicious circle, it may be tempting for the practitioner to go along with the labeling process of the identified client (e.g., oppositional defiant disorder) and then use that label as a reason for participants in the circle to change some of their actions and behaviors. While this is often necessary in the sense of helping a client or family qualify for intervention, this practice does not seem ethical unless the practitioner is willing to consider his or her own behavior as possibly being a part of the vicious circle. The practitioner's willingness to include him or herself in the circle's diagnosis of one person should only be done tentatively and with supervisory input, to ensure that the practitioner's efforts to help do not become a sustained part of the system's problem.

When the vicious circle sequence is noted or suspected but moves at a slow rate of speed, the practitioner's first intervention may include a speeding up of the process, so that it can be witnessed and dealt with in its entirety. The faster the speed of the vicious circle sequence, the more likely appropriate change measures can be implemented. The speed of the circle can be increased by adding more individuals to the session who are players in the circle, or by actually asking the client to escalate his or her production of symptomatic behavior (Greene, 1996; Lantz, 1978). This is also known as a paradoxical approach to problem resolution. For example, the child who acts out to "rescue" his parents from having to deal with each other by arguing with a younger sibling may be asked to misbehave more frequently (only in ways that will not create new problems for the child). When the rate or speed of the vicious circle is increased, there will be an increase in the availability of assessment data and, more importantly, a decrease in the stability of the vicious circle sequence.

SUMMARY

This chapter has discussed the vicious circle as a common and potentially unifying concept that may help to explain how different theoretical approaches may work in short-term intervention. The vicious circle was broken down into different elements, including composition (individual, dyadic, and triadic), type (snowball and homeostatic), form, speed, and territory. A set of assessment and intervention guidelines for use in breaking up vicious cycles was also presented.

6

Race and Culture in Short-Term Existential Intervention

BEGINNING IN THE LATE 1960S AND EARLY 1970S CLINICAL PRACTITIONERS became aware of the impact of race and culture on their work (Harper & Lantz, 1996). Many articles and books have been published since then outlining how some traditional practice methods have not been pertinent to minority race and culture clients and in fact have often been damaging (Lee, 2002). Many practitioners have recommended a modification of traditional clinical practice methods in working with minority clients, and others have even suggested that majority race and middle-class clinical practitioners should not work with minority clients. In short-term existential intervention, practice with clients from a different culture, class, or race is both potentially useful and potentially damaging (Lantz, 2002). It is potentially useful because the differences between the helper and client can facilitate increased knowledge, insight, coping skills, meaning potentials, and opportunities in the lives of both parties. It is potentially dangerous if the practitioner does not have cultural sensitivity and specific knowledge about the client's cultural values, social functioning patterns, values, and worldview. This chapter outlines major themes in transcultural intervention to help the existential practitioner ensure that he or she does not overlook important aspects of clients' life and problem experiences.

TRANSCULTURAL INTERVENTION

There are four types of short-term existential intervention situations that can be described as transcultural. These situations are a dominant culture (e.g., white) practitioner and a minority culture (e.g., African American) client, a minority culture practitioner and a majority culture client, a minority culture client and a different minority culture practitioner, and a majority culture practitioner and majority culture client who come from similar cultural backgrounds but have experienced a different process of acculturation in their families of origin (Harper & Lantz, 1996; Lantz, 2000). Although it is possible to conduct effective intervention in all the above situations, it should be noted that the greater the cultural differences between client and practitioner, the greater the difficulty the parties will have in developing a facilitative treatment relationship (Lee, 2002; Lum, 1999).

It is important to emphasize that, perhaps contrary to what one might expect, research on the effects of similarities and differences between practitioners and their clients on intervention outcomes does *not* support matching on such variables as age, gender, sexual orientation, race, or ethnicity. Instead, clients want to work with practitioners who are experienced and who have knowledge of relevant cultural differences between them. This is consistently found in research studies regarding gender (Hatchet & Park, 2004; Parker-Sloat, 2003), sexual orientation (Burckell & Goldfriend, 2006), Hispanic clients and Anglo practitioners (Flicker, 2005), Asian American clients and Caucasian practitioners (Ito & Marimba, 2002), and African American clients and Caucasian practitioners (Negy, 2004; Liu, 2004; Sherman, 2000). Clients desire practitioners with cultural competency and sensitivity, rather than cultural sameness.

The four types of practitioner/client characteristics in transcultural intervention will now be discussed.

Dominant Culture Practitioner and Minority Culture Client

In this transcultural clinical situation a client from a minority race or culture is provided with crisis intervention services by a member of the dominant culture (in the United States this generally means a Caucasian practitioner). In this situation there is often a great difference in the worldviews of the parties, which in turn gives rise to opportunities for misunderstanding, distraction, and prejudice (Congress, 1997; Harper & Lantz, 1996; Van Voorhis, 1998). In such situations the existential practitioner is responsible for:

◆ Actively researching and developing knowledge about the client's culture and race
◆ Actively engaging the client in the practitioner's self-education process by asking questions and being open to the client's efforts to help the practitioner improve his or her understanding of the client's heritage
◆ Utilizing self-analysis skills to monitor and evaluate his or her own possible distortions, transferences, and prejudices about the client's cultural and racial heritage (Congress, 1997; Harper & Lantz, 1996; Lee, 2002; Van Voorhis, 1998).

The practitioner's research of practice guidelines must involve learning about the characteristics of the ethnic group of which the client is a member. Members of ethnic groups often have unique perspectives on themselves, the world, and the nature of clinical intervention. In one instance of existential intervention on a college campus, the practitioner, a middle-aged Caucasian male from a small midwestern city, was working with a twenty-one-year-old client named Connie who originally came from Puerto Rico by way of New York City. Following the intake he reviewed two textbooks for information about persons from Puerto Rico (Fong & Furuto,

2001; Green, 1999). The practitioner learned that Puerto Ricans are the second-largest Latino subgroup in the United States. Their culture emphasizes spirituality (sometimes outside the frame of formal religion), the importance of extended and cross-generational family ties, and the values of community, children, respect, and cooperation. Interestingly, and significant to his client's presentation, Latino children tend to have a heightened sensitivity to the nonverbal behaviors of others. Latino people also value personalism in relationships—informality and warmth rather than observances of formal roles.

Interestingly, the practitioner recognized over time that Connie displayed some personality characteristics that were different from what might be expected of a woman with a strong Puerto Rican ethnic background. She certainly was sensitive to nonverbal behaviors and maintained an informal relationship with the practitioner, but on the other hand, her family background featured conflict and splintering rather than the close ties that are characteristic of Puerto Rican families. Connie had also moved far away from her extended family, and she was willing to seek mental health treatment, when it is often observed that those with Puerto Rican origins are more likely to get help from spiritual advisors or medical doctors (Garcia-Preto, 1996). Furthermore, the client did not seem guided by a spiritual frame of reference. Thus, while understanding the client's unique cultural background was important, the practitioner learned that he must be careful not to use this information to stereotype the client.

Minority Practitioner and Dominant Culture Client

In this clinical situation a minority culture practitioner provides crisis intervention services to a client from the dominant culture. The minority culture practitioner may discover that client distortions about the practitioner's culture, or simple client prejudice, threaten to disrupt the intervention process. The minority culture practitioner is thus responsible for monitoring and utilizing client distortions to help the majority culture client gain a more accurate view of the practitioner's world. The practitioner may also have to overcome or control damaged feelings that have resulted from episodes of prejudice and discrimination by dominant culture people in the past. The minority culture practitioner's task is to remain professional even if the dominant culture client is treating him or her in an unfair manner (Harper & Lantz, 1996).

Minority Culture Practitioner and Minority Culture Client

In this clinical situation a minority culture practitioner and a client from a different minority culture attempt to work together to develop an adequate treatment relationship and working alliance. Minority culture practitioners are sometimes surprised at how difficult it can be to connect with members of a different minority group, because they may assume that being from a minority group gives them special insight into the differences of living in any minority culture. The truth is, of course, that people from different minority cultures and races all face special problems in a heterogeneous society, and comparing minority culture situations often results in inaccurate assumptions (Lantz, 1978; Lee, 2002). In this clinical situation the minority culture practitioner may exhibit adequate cultural sensitivity but inadequate cultural knowledge of the client and the client's cultural heritage. The practitioner must be aware of his or her responsibility to learn about the unique characteristics of each different minority group encountered in practice, in much the same way that was described earlier.

Majority Culture Practitioner and Majority Culture Client

It is sometimes assumed that when a majority culture practitioner is working with a majority culture client, this cannot be considered to be a transcultural clinical helping situation. This is an incorrect assumption because the similarities between client and practitioner that appear on a surface level often cloud awareness of differences that might disrupt the quality of the intervention process (Harper & Lantz, 1996). Such differences are likely to be present because skin color is not always the primary culture determinant. Every cultural movement has within it many different migrating paths, and every culture and racial heritage incorporates differences based on religious heterogeneity, migration path differences, family history, and historical accident.

In summary, it is most constructive to assume that *every* practice situation is a transcultural clinical situation.

UNDERSTANDING CULTURALLY COMPETENT PRACTICE

Mo Yee Lee and her colleagues at the Ohio State University College of Social Work (Lee, 2000, 2002; Lee & Green, 2002) have developed a transcultural education model that can be used to educate clinical practitioners about effective cross-cultural practice. This model is particularly relevant for the practice of short-term existential intervention. In Lee's model, two dimensions of competence, cultural knowledge and cultural sensitivity, are the primary factors involved in providing effective transcultural intervention (figure 6.1).

Cultural knowledge refers to the practitioner's ability to acquire specific knowledge about his or her clients':

◆ Cultural background
◆ Racial experiences
◆ Historical experiences
◆ Values
◆ Behaviors
◆ Attitudes
◆ Spiritual beliefs
◆ Worldview beliefs

Figure 6.1. Competence in transcultural clinical intervention. Adapted with modification from M. Lee (2002): *Working with Asian American populations: A treatment guide.* Columbus, OH: Asian American Community Services.

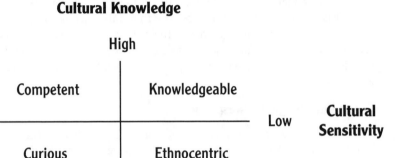

Cultural Knowledge

High

Competent	Knowledgeable

High ——————————————————— Low   **Cultural Sensitivity**

Curious	Ethnocentric

Low

- ◆ Resources
- ◆ Customs
- ◆ Educational experiences
- ◆ Communication patterns
- ◆ Analysis patterns
- ◆ Thinking patterns
- ◆ Coping skills
- ◆ Previous experiences when requesting help in a dominant culture setting (Harper & Lantz, 1996; Lee, 2002).

Cultural sensitivity refers to a person's attitudes and values about cross-cultural direct service practice and about people from different cultures and racial groups (Lee, 2002). In transcultural intervention it is hoped that the practitioner will manifest cultural sensitivity by developing the qualities of openness, empathy, respect, acceptance, and flexibility when working with people of a different race or culture.

The factors of cultural knowledge and cultural sensitivity can be utilized together (see figure 6.1) to identify four potential personal responses to the transcultural practice situation that are sometimes manifested by existential practitioners. These responses can be identified as the *ethnocentric* response, the *knowledgeable* response, the *curious* response and the *competent* response.

The Ethnocentric Response

In this response to the transcultural practice situation the practitioner has a low degree of cultural knowledge about his or her clients and also manifests little cultural sensitivity or empathy for the client. The ethnocentric practitioner manifests little motivation to either gain increased cultural knowledge or cultural sensitivity and holds to the worldview that his or her own cultural practices are superior to those of people from different cultural or racial groups. A practitioner from any racial group, gender, gender preference, or cultural heritage can manifest such a response. Ethnocentric practitioners believe that difference is dangerous, and they are not frequently motivated to change their stance. It can be concluded that ethnocentric people do not function well as clinical practitioners. All clients deserve a practitioner who is, if not sensitive and knowledgeable, at least willing to grow in those ways.

The Knowledgeable Response

In the knowledgeable response to the transcultural situation the practitioner is willing to expand his or her knowledge and awareness about different cultures, worldviews, and patterns of coping and growth. Although the knowledgeable practitioner generally has a high level of cultural knowledge, he or she also has a low level of cultural sensitivity. Such practitioners often resort to the use of stereotypes when working with minority culture clients, as they utilize knowledge about general minority client patterns to avoid contact and empathic concern with specific minority clients. The knowledgeable practitioner requires close supervision but is often able to grow into a more culturally sensitive and competent practitioner over time. Below is a vignette that demonstrates the problems that may ensue when a practitioner assumes the knowledgeable response.

A Caucasian male practitioner at a mental health agency occasionally felt uncomfortable with African American male clients. The practitioner did not think of himself as racist, but he understood that racial differences could negatively affect practitioners and their clients. He always raised the issue of racial difference with new clients when it existed to see if they had concerns about it. Usually his clients did not express any reservations. The practitioner's problem, though, is that he was reluctant to raise the issue of race again during the intervention if he perceived that it might be a barrier between the client and himself. He didn't want to risk insulting the client or imply that he was preoccupied with race.

Leon was a middle-aged and unemployed single African American male who came to the agency because of severe depression related to chronic job problems, conflicts with women, and a recently strained relationship with his domineering father. He was rather well known around town as a talented jazz pianist. During the first session he raised the issue of race himself, seeming suspicious that the practitioner might not be able to understand his life experiences. It was a constructive conversation and they both seemed satisfied with its outcome. Every so often, though, he would challenge the practitioner again, wondering openly if he could empathize with him. This became difficult, because the practitioner did think that in many situations the client placed himself in the victim role more than the evidence warranted, using race as an excuse. But the practitioner was not comfortable saying this because he was not sure that his perceptions were valid. Leon dropped out of intervention after three visits. The practitioner suspected that Leon questioned his awareness of, and comfort in addressing, the African American experience. The practitioner decided afterward that he needed to learn more about managing differences with his clients.

The Curious Response

In the curious response the practitioner has high cultural sensitivity and low knowledge about minority culture clients. The practitioner is highly motivated to learn more about minority culture clients' reactions to his or her basic cultural sensitivity and ability to develop empathy for the client. This is an open response that craves knowledge, and the practitioner is highly motivated to use his or her knowledge in clinical work with minority culture clients. Such practitioners are able to effectively utilize books and articles about minority culture clients for their professional growth.

The Competent Response

The competent response to the transcultural helping situation involves high cultural knowledge and high cultural sensitivity. In addition to acquiring considerable culture-specific knowledge about minority culture clients, the competent practitioner demonstrates openness, empathy, and care with minority cultural clients and is able to maintain an informed and empathic response to them. The competent response to the cross-cultural helping situation should be a primary educational goal in the graduate education experiences of all helping professions and should also be a primary goal in competent clinical supervision. When a practitioner has developed a competent response to the transcultural helping situation, he or she is able to make sound clinical judgments from an informed point of view, is open and sensitive in the cross-cultural helping situation, is not bound by conceptual knowledge, can connect with a client at an individual empathic level, is aware of the potential for his or her own personal experiences to distort judgment in the transcultural helping situation, and is able to step outside the self in order to view the minority client from a multiperspective frame of reference.

SUMMARY

Almost all forms of existential intervention can be understood as transcultural helping. In this chapter a number of transcultural clinical situations are described, as well as the four primary patterns of response that may be manifested by helping professionals in the transcultural clinical situation. The process of competent transcultural helping has also been described. This chapter ends with another case vignette, a first-person account that illustrates a competent response to the transcultural helping situation,

THE APACHE TEAR

Rebecca, age forty, came to my mental health agency to get help with anxiety and depression. She was a recovering cocaine abuser but experienced so much anxiety that she was physically ill, feeling light-headed and nauseous every day. Rebecca was tormented, worrying about the physical and emotional welfare of her adoptive father and brother and her ability to stay free of drugs. Her anxiety seemed to be rooted in a fear that she was going to lose control of her life. To prevent this she tried to be perfect, in complete control, because she had been so out of control several years earlier.

Rebecca, a Native American, was born on an Indian reservation in the western United States. Her parents gave her up for adoption when she was seven. Her adoptive parents were white but they encouraged Rebecca to stay involved with her Indian culture. She visited her natural father every year on the reservation and interacted with Native American groups in her current area of residence. I wondered if it would be difficult for Rebecca to work with me, a white female, but the racial difference did not appear to be a barrier. This was largely because I asked her to help me understand her culture, and I read several books about her Apache tribe. I often shared with Rebecca what I learned from my reading, and she seemed to enjoy helping me in this way. I also talked with my supervisor often about my work with this client, to help ensure that I was not overlooking anything important as a result of our differences. Rebecca and I worked together for about six sessions, and she learned to control her anxiety through a variety of reflective and behavioral activities. She made excellent progress.

When we met for the last time, Rebecca presented me with a polished gemstone, a smooth, dark stone that she called an "Apache tear." The stone was dark but became transparent when held up to light, and a small "tear" could be seen in its center. The stone had been given to her by a friend many years before, and she wanted to pass it on to me. She explained that the Apache tear symbolized both struggle and one's hopes for a better future. She said that she had been struggling for years, but now she could look ahead with confidence and self-acceptance. She wanted to give me the stone as a thank you. She added that she had the stone blessed by a tribal healer before bringing it to me.

We spent a fair amount of time during our final session talking about the Apache tear. I thought it was a wonderful gesture. It was very important to my client to give me the gift and also to explain its history and significance. Agency policies often prohibit or discourage clinical staff from accepting gifts from clients. Sometimes, though, it is important for the client to give a gift and refusing it would be destructive to the relationship. I will treasure that stone forever.

Part 2

Applications

7

Re-collection Interventions with Older Adults

OLD AGE POSES IMPORTANT EXISTENTIAL CHALLENGES FOR PEOPLE, IN-cluding coming to terms with the transitory nature of life, coping with the approach of death, enduring illness and suffering, being confronted with ultimate meaning and religious questions, and managing the problems of loneliness, anxiety, and depression (Langle & Probst, 2004). The older adult may thus require an enhanced ability to respond to the fundamental questions of existence. This chapter reviews one major existential intervention strategy, *re-collection,* that is useful in helping older adults to manage these challenges.

Re-collection is a form of honoring suppressed meaning potentials that the client is able to make real once again (as described in chapter 3). This helps the client to manifest existence at the being for the world dimension. Honoring is a celebration of the older adult client's renewed ability to hold, tell, and master those meanings that were once most significant to his or her life.

Viktor Frankl's approach to psychotherapy holds that many (although not all) emotional problems develop in order to fill the existential vacuum that occurs when a person is not able to experience a sense of meaning and purpose in life (Frankl, 1969, 2000). The primary function of the practitioner in these instances is to help the client:

◆ Notice meaning potentials and opportunities in the future
◆ Discover actualization methods that can be used in the here and now to make use of meaning potentials
◆ Re-collect and honor meanings previously actualized, but deposited in the past (Frankl, 1969, 1975; Lantz, 1974, 1989, 1995).

Through these processes the client can fill the existential vacuum with a renewed sense of purpose and decrease the intensity and frequency of psychiatric symptoms that have grown there.

The three basic curative factors involved in this process are noticing, actualizing, and re-collection. Although all three of these are useful interventions, the purpose of this chapter is to focus on the curative factor of *re-collection* during short-term existential intervention with older adults. Such a focus may have value in expanding the understanding of reminiscence therapy approaches to mental health interventions with older adults.

To begin this discussion, general information about reminiscence and related therapies is provided. Reminiscence and validation therapies, which stimulate a client's memory and mood in the context of systematically discussing events in his or her life history, have been shown in several studies to improve short-term mood, behavior, and cognition (Burnside & Haight, 1994; Nomura, 2002). Reality orientation and skills training, which are used to increase the client's awareness of the present and ability to focus on self-care, also seem to have modest benefits, although these gains do not always persist beyond the situation in which they are applied (Metiteri, Zanetti, Geroldi, Frisoni, DeLeo, et al., 2001; Williams, 1994). It is important to note that these two interventions may have some possible adverse effects when they do not address the unique situation of a client, including increased agitation and frustration in clients and the caregivers who work with them.

Recreational and art therapies provide stimulation and enrichment for older adults who are depressed or have memory problems, as they help to mobilize clients' cognitive processes. These interventions seem to produce short-term improvements in mood and decreases in behavioral problems (Fitzsimmons & Buettner, 2003; Rovner, Steel, Shmuely, & Folstein, 1996). Data on their effectiveness is limited, but they are widely accepted as appropriate common-sense interventions. One group of researchers has developed a behavioral protocol for managing clients with memory problems that offers a variety of pleasant activities, a process that improves the overall moods of both clients and caregivers (Teri, 1994; Teri & Logsdon, 1991).

The contributions of the existential perspective to reminiscence and related interventions will now be discussed.

FRANKL'S CONCEPT OF TIME

The concept of time is an important aspect of Frankl's (1955, 1969) intervention approach. In his concept of time, emphasis is placed on the importance of the client's past, which then provides an enriched understanding of both the future and the here and now. The past is a storehouse or museum for meanings that clients have actualized and made forever real, although they may exist out of consciousness at the present time (Frankl, 1975; Lantz, 1974; Lantz & Ahern, 1994). Although it may be suppressed, the past represents existence that can never be destroyed. The three curative factors described above, and their relationship to time, are listed in table 7.1.

This relationship between time and intervention can be summarized thus:

◆ The past is the storehouse for meanings that have been actualized and made forever real, whether or not they are within the client's awareness in the present.

Table 7.1. Curative factors and their relationship to time

Element of Time	Curative Factor
The future	Noticing
The present	Actualizing
The past	Re-collecting

♦ The present is the time to actualize and make use of meaning potentials.
♦ The future includes meaning potentials to be noticed.

In Frankl's view, to forget the past always involves forgetting the meanings that a person has actualized and made forever real. This creates an existential-meaning vacuum in which symptoms of emotional and behavioral problems may develop and persist. Thus, helping a client remember the meanings that have been deposited in the past is a helpful way of shrinking the client's existential vacuum and the symptoms that grow there. This process of helping the client recover, remember, and rediscover meanings previously actualized is known as *re-collection*, or honoring (Lantz, 1974, 1995). In this process the existential practitioner may utilize both reflective and expressive activities to help the client become aware of the meanings that have been repressed, denied, or forgotten. Re-collection can be used with any types of client but in this chapter it is presented as an effective tool for working with older adults.

Figure 7.1 illustrates the process of re-collection in existential therapy with older adults.

INDUCTIVE AND DEDUCTIVE ASPECTS OF RE-COLLECTION WITH OLDER ADULTS

The process of re-collection in short-term existential intervention represents both a deductive and an inductive process. It is a deductive, theory-based process in the sense that it is squarely based on Frankl's (1969) theory of "existenzanalyse." In this theory it is accepted that the process of re-collection will always help a client decrease the intensity of both the existential-meaning vacuum and the symptoms that grow in that vacuum (Frankl, 1975; Lantz, 1995). It is also an inductive process, because during the process of reflection the practitioner cannot know in advance what the client will remember, nor the kinds of meanings the client will uncover. The practitioner must be alert to signs that the client is reflecting on an important meaning issue and be willing to validate whatever is uncovered.

It is important to understand that every human being is called by life to actualize and make use of unique, individually specific meaning potentials. For Frankl (1959, 1969), all of us are responsible to answer the call of such unique meaning potentials. It is therefore impossible to deductively (or objectively) understand or predict the unique meanings that an older adult has actualized and deposited in the

Figure 7.1. Re-collection in intervention with older adults.

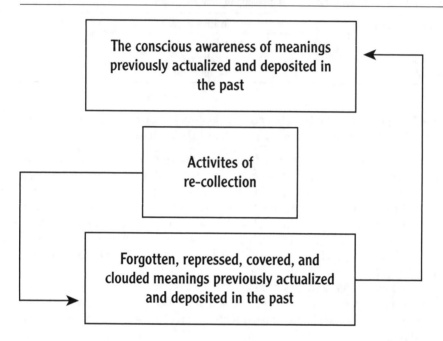

past, and which are available for re-collection. Frankl also points out that whenever we assume that we know the meanings in another person's life, we may become biased and blind to the authentic meanings in that person's life. Knowledge of the other person can only be discovered with any validity through a patient process of inductive dialogue, facilitated through the use of such techniques as dream reflection, poetry, and looking at photographs.

The following clinical illustrations provide examples of how re-collection can be used in the practice of short-term existential intervention.

FACILITATING DISCUSSION TOWARD RE-COLLECTION

Mr. Miller was an Irish American man who was referred for short-term existential intervention by a nurse at a hospice agency in central Ohio. Mr. Miller had been told that he had terminal cancer. He was receiving pain medications, social service assistance, and nursing services to help him and his wife face his cancer and upcoming death with dignity in their own home. Mr. Miller had been worrying his helpers and his wife with an unprecedented and continuous desire to talk about his experiences in World War II as a South Pacific combat infantryman. He seemed to be preoccupied with this part of his life, almost to the exclusion of everything else. The hospice staff did not understand "why this stuff is so important to Mr. Miller."

The existential practitioner's work focused on helping Mr. Miller to reflect, remember, and talk about his World War II combat experiences. The practitioner used open-ended questions, reflective comments, and sincere personal interest to help Mr. Miller re-collect and honor the meanings that he and his soldier friends had actualized and made real during World War II. This was a part of the client's life about which he was particularly proud. He had made a strong connection to other people (his fellow soldiers) and felt that he was making a significant contribution to an important cause.

Mr. Miller was not deemphasizing the love he felt for his family, but he had never before shared with them the stories of his war days. He wanted to do so before he died. Mr. Miller found it especially helpful to tell his stories to his wife, his two adult sons, and his oldest granddaughter in two conjoint family therapy sessions, held during the week of his death. He wanted his family to understand the experiences that made him who he was. Mr. Miller's family members were receptive to hearing his stories, especially after the practitioner explained to them why the process was so important to Mr. Miller.

The practitioner assumed the role of mediator in these conversations. His manner was calm and comforting. He encouraged each family member to participate in the conversations, allowed each person to speak without interruption, clarified each person's unclear statements, and affirmed the importance of each member's remarks. After these two sessions Mr. Miller reported that he was no longer afraid of death because he would soon be joining those soldier friends he had known as a young adult in heaven. Mr. Miller expressed gratitude to the crisis practitioner for taking his past seriously and "honoring my life."

ART AS RE-COLLECTION

Mrs. Johnson was a seventy-eight-year-old African American widow who was admitted to an assisted-living residential center due to an inability to manage her activities of daily living. She initially avoided contact with other residents whenever possible, using isolation strategies. Still, she reported to several staff members that she felt empty and alone and was having problems finding any meaning in her life. Mrs. Jackson eventually agreed to participate in an art reflection group that was held three times weekly in her assisted-living residence.

The assisted-living staff noticed a major positive change in Mrs. Jackson's mood and functioning patterns after a particular art reflection activity that occurred in the group. The activities therapist asked the group members one day to draw the "most beautiful sunset you have ever seen in your life." Mrs. Jackson produced a drawing of herself, her husband, and their daughter watching a sunset in the Smokey Mountains. Mrs. Jackson reported to the group during the follow-up discussion that she had observed this sunset on a family vacation and that it was one of many sunsets they saw in the Smokies. Mrs. Jackson's sunset drawing triggered the memory of many beautiful experiences with her husband and her daughter. The art reflection group and the expressive art activities helped Mrs. Jackson to reminisce, remember, and re-collect many of the nature and family meanings she had forgotten. She was able to recall that she had taken advantage of many opportunities to see the world, and that her life had been productive and meaningful in giving life and sustenance to her family. She was able to recall that she was a person who still liked contributing to the well-being of other people, and this gave her present life a sense of added significance.

POETRY AS RE-COLLECTION

Poetry may be useful in helping a client uncover repressed meanings and meaning potentials in the existential unconscious (Frankl, 1978; Harper & Lantz, 1996). This can be addressed in three ways. At times, the practitioner may give the older adult selected poetry to read that may stir the re-collection of meanings lost in the past. At other times the practitioner can encourage the older adult client to write his or her own poem to facilitate re-collection. For some older adult clients, it is useful for the practitioner to write a poem about the client's life and give it to the client as a way of facilitating the re-collection process. The three methods of using poetry have been shown to be helpful (Harper & Lantz, 1996). Due to its unique formats, writing poetry provides a new way of thinking about oneself and one's life, as it helps to free up the person from habitual ways of thinking about him or herself. Poetry may help a person to tap into suppressed thoughts and feelings that have tended to elude thought.

Mrs. Lopez was a seventy-three-year-old Latina woman who lived with her daughter and son-in-law in a modest home in a large midwestern city. She loved her family but had become increasingly despondent about her waning physical strength and concurrent inability to maintain many of her household responsibilities and personal interest activities, such as daily walks. Fortunately her eyesight was excellent. Mrs. Lopez felt bored and useless, and her daughter called the local mental health agency when her mother began having crying spells. The existential practitioner who visited the home determined that Mrs. Lopez was sinking into a serious depression related in part to a lack of purpose in her life. In addition to ensuring that the woman received a thorough physical and ongoing medical care through his case management brokerage and referral activities, the practitioner encouraged her to begin reading poetry after he learned during his assessment that she loved the work of Pablo Neruda.

Her daughter had forgotten that Mrs. Lopez had once loved literature. The practitioner encouraged the family to make a trip to the local library, where they checked out several of Neruda's works. Mrs. Lopez read them with pleasure and discussed them with the practitioner during each of his four home visits. The poetry reminded her of the Latin culture and put her back into touch with many cultural aspects of her parents' world that meant so much to her, but which had become diluted after so many years in the United States. Mrs. Lopez not only began reading more as a pastime, but she regained a sense of pride in the beauty of her cultural background. Her crying spells diminished, and she was able to continue living with her family with greater satisfaction.

PHOTOGRAPHS AS RE-COLLECTION

Mrs. Norris was an attractive, wealthy seventy-six-year-old widowed woman with three grown, successful children who lived in a luxurious apartment in a high-rise apartment building. Her son-in-law referred her for short-term existential intervention. Mrs. Norris was suffering from depression and was not able to appreciate or enjoy her many achievements in her life. Mrs. Norris reported that she had gotten negative about everything since her husband died a few years ago.

Intervention with Mrs. Norris was two-pronged. On one hand she was evaluated and placed on an antidepressant medication by the practitioner's psychiatric consultant. Mrs. Norris responded well to medication and found herself with more energy, more joy, less confusion, and an increased desire to get out and get more involved. Her existential intervention involved re-collection work using photographs. In the initial stage of the intervention, the practitioner had instructed Mrs. Norris to bring a sample of photographs to their sessions. She was asked to pick out fifty or sixty photographs that showed important and meaningful events throughout her life. Mrs. Norris was then asked to separate the photos into three separate piles. The first pile was for photographs that showed pleasurable experiences that Mrs. Norris had taken from the world. This pile represented what Frankl (1955, 1969) has identified as experiential meanings. A second pile was for photographs that showed and represented products and gifts that Mrs. Norris had given to the world. This pile represented creative or productive meanings. The third pile was for photographs that represented periods and situations of Mrs. Norris' life where she utilized integrity and defiance to stand up for her values and beliefs, or to confront a tragedy or other painful circumstance. This pile of photographs represented defiant or empowerment meanings (Lee, 1996).

During each of their five meetings, Mrs. Norris and the practitioner reviewed the photographs in each pile and Mrs. Norris told the story behind each one. Mrs. Norris felt that such an opportunity for re-collection was extremely helpful. She insisted that the process of photograph re-collection helped her "get back my memories and my pride." Mrs. Norris took the initiative to end the intervention. She continued to occasionally visit her psychiatrist, although her medication was discontinued one year after she was clear of her symptoms of depression. The medications helped Mrs. Norris regain equilibrium, and the re-collection helped her obtain existential growth.

SUMMARY

The process of re-collection or honoring in short-term existential intervention is an effective method of helping older adults shrink both the existential-meaning vacuum and the symptoms that grow in the existential vacuum. The use of discussion, art, poetry, and photographs are all methods of facilitating re-collection that are useful in working with older adults. Re-collection helps the older adult remember, find, discover, and honor previously actualized meanings that have been forgotten and lost in the past.

This chapter closes with a vignette that describes a type of re-collection with an older adult that surprised the practitioner.

THE LIFE THAT MIGHT HAVE BEEN

I worked as a member of an oncology care team in Vermont. We provided counseling and social services for persons with life-threatening cancer. I worked with the team for two and a half years, but then I enrolled in graduate school in Boston and had to leave. I began sharing the news with my clients a few months before I left. In that program I was accustomed to ending with clients when they passed away—the fact that I was the one leaving was ironic.

I had known Rose, a widow in her mid-seventies, for more than one year, and despite her cancer she was getting along well and might survive for another year or more. We had a good relationship. She was in the hospital for chemotherapy treatments when I told her about my leaving. I expected that Rose would be upset, and view my departure as a blow to her support system, but she surprised me! When I told her of my plans, her first reaction was excitement. She thought it was wonderful that I was moving on with my life and career. She asked about the details of my move to Boston. Rose had spent her entire life in rural Vermont. She had a good life and a great family, but I realized that day that a part of her wondered how her life might have been different if she had left home and seen more of the world.

Professionals who work with older adults know that at the end of one's life the sense of identity and meaning may be affirmed by telling his or her story of her life and perhaps re-collecting meanings from the past. Rose undertook a different kind of life review with me. She talked not about her life, but what her life might have been like if she had moved away from Vermont as a young woman. It occurred to me that she saw me as having the kind of life she might have had if she had been born fifty years later. Still, as she talked about my future, she reaffirmed for herself that, in spite of what she had missed, she had lived a satisfying life, finding meaning in the commitments she had made within her rural environment.

I wrote a letter to Rose after I got settled in Boston, letting her know where I was living and how my new life as a graduate student in the big city was getting underway. I knew that it would be important for her to get that news from me.

8

Play and Art Interventions with Children and Their Parents

THIS CHAPTER DISCUSSES THE USES OF SHORT-TERM EXISTENTIAL IN-tervention with children and illustrates the utility of play and art as intervention strategies. Children may use arts-based methods of coping with the struggles in their lives, and such expression allows a healthy detachment from those struggles (Matto, Corcoran, & Fassler, 2003). This chapter does not address intervention in situations where children are living with parents who have abused or neglected them. Rather, the discussion is limited to situations where the child has been trauma-tized outside the family, or when the abused child is living in a safe foster family after experiencing abuse at the hands of the natural parents.

See figure 3.1 for a review of the process of short-term existential intervention, and the steps of holding, telling, mastering, and honoring. Consistent with that pro-cess, the following sections of this chapter describe how traumatized children and their parents can use play and art to:

◆ Hold up trauma pain to conscious awareness
◆ Tell each other and the practitioner the story of their trauma pain
◆ Find ways to master the trauma pain
◆ Find ways to give to the world in honoring their trauma experiences

PLAY AND ART THERAPY

This section begins with a brief overview of play therapy (Ablon, 1996; Tsao, 2002). A child's ability to engage in play is essential for his or her development in the areas of cognition, language, social behavior, emotional behavior, and problem-solving skills. Play can also allow a child to experience a sense of freedom, control, and mastery, which can lead to a sense of empowerment.

Various psychology theorists such as Freud, Erikson, and Vygotsky have ad-dressed the importance of play. Freud believed play can help release negative feel-ings caused by traumatic events and substitute more positive feelings for them. Children can come to understand painful situations and find ways to substitute unpleasant feelings with pleasurable ones. Play can also help children reduce their fears of abandonment and vulnerability. Erikson suggested that play can help children develop their self-esteem and sense of empowerment by allowing mastery of objects, which can in turn lead to their mastery of peer interactions. Vygotsky theorized that play can help children develop capacities for self-regulation and abstract thinking. Children can learn through play, and various play materials can help in that learning. For example, a puzzle may help a child learn that there is only one way to solve a problem, whereas blocks may show a child that creativity can help him or her uncover more than one way to solve a problem. Therefore, giving children various play materials to provide the creative spark is important.

In a therapeutic setting, play can powerfully facilitate development, even with a minimum amount of verbalization and interpretation. It is not always necessary to provide insight or to verbally structure a play therapy session. The child may produce many drawings without discussing them, play board games without discussing how they may be related to his or her life, or even remain silent while perusing books or magazines. Being able to express him or herself in these ways in a safe environment can be therapeutic for the child. Thus, play therapy can be different from a practitioner's traditional methods of clarification and interpretation. The child may eventually bring forward and explore troublesome feelings. The child may also express and communicate feelings without the practitioner's reflective comments. The practitioner must be able to "sit" with the child at times. More active interventions may (perhaps unconsciously) serve to allow the child to avoid experiencing or expressing painful feelings, which may be difficult for the practitioner to tolerate as well. That is, the practitioner's difficulty with tolerating negative affect can lead to his or her defensive efforts of intellectualization, premature intervention, manipulation, limit setting, and other activities that may inhibit the child's productive explorations. It is important to bear with the child by having empathetic appreciation of his or her internal feelings.

The application of play and art therapy in the context of short-term existential intervention will now be considered.

HOLDING, PLAY, AND ART WITH TRAUMATIZED CHILDREN AND PARENTS

Holding refers to the use of the treatment relationship to help traumatized children and their parents bring repressed feelings, memories, problems, and conflicts from the unconscious to the conscious level of awareness (Lantz, 1993; Lantz & Raiz, 2003). Through holding, the existential practitioner lends the traumatized child and the parents an empathic self to create an intervention structure that facilitates awareness, disclosure, and insight about the trauma situation. This structure contributes to the child and parents' sense of increased safety and support, and a decreased level of anxiety about awareness and disclosure (Gil, 1991; Golan, 1978; Lantz, 2000; Moon, 1990). This process is illustrated in the situation of Billy Smith and his parents.

SAND PLAY

Sand play is a means of helping a client access unconscious material and make it conscious by giving it form. It can reduce symptoms of emotional trauma, anxiety, aggression, and even physical pain. This activity encourages children and families to express, contain, and symbolize their emotions. This intervention technique has cross-cultural utility as well, as in situations where traditional values dictate personal reserve and nonverbal healing techniques rather than open sharing about troubling thoughts and feelings.

In sand play, the practitioner provides a large tray of sand and several objects that can represent people in the client's life (Sullivan, 2003; Vaz, 2000). The client (and perhaps other participants) is asked to construct a certain life scenario or perhaps is given no directives at all. During sand play, the practitioner provides relatively few interpretations of what is going on and instead acts as an empathetic witness to the child's experience and healing. The process is considered complete only when the images in the client's tray reflect a return to a more effective approach to life.

THE SMITH FAMILY

Nine-year-old Billy and his parents were referred for intervention after another child at the school reported that he and Billy had been molested by a young adult male volunteer. Billy was unable to say that he had been molested, saying only that he had forgotten what happened. Billy was eventually able to remember and disclose what had happened after the practitioner encouraged Billy and his parents to use a sand play experience to practice protecting a small boy doll.

In Billy's sand play experience the practitioner put a small boy doll in the middle of the sand tray and told Billy and his parents that their job was to practice protecting the doll. The practitioner asked Mrs. Smith to place a small mother figurine next to the boy doll if she was willing to protect the boy. Mrs. Smith said she was and put her figurine next to the boy doll. Mr. Smith followed this lead and put a father figurine next to the boy doll. The practitioner placed a fairy godmother figurine behind the parent figures to give them even more power. Billy built a fence around the boy doll, the parent figurines, and the fairy godmother. The practitioner then asked the family to identify relatives and friends who could be trusted and to put them outside the fence to help protect the family and the fairy godmother. The family members took turns remembering who could be trusted and placing a figurine in the sand tray to help guard the fairy and the family. Mrs. Smith called the practitioner the next day and reported that Billy had remembered what happened to him and had told her the details of the episode.

PLAY, ART, AND TELLING

Telling refers to the intervention strategy that helps the traumatized child and his or her parents to disclose their trauma experiences and pain to each other and to the practitioner (Lantz, 2002; Tick, 2001). Telling is an important treatment element, as it transforms trauma pain from an internal experience into a dyadic or triadic interactional experience of pain that is then made available for encounter support (Lantz & Gyamerah, 2002). Telling trauma pain to other family members allows them to help the client fill in the gaps of the story, tell the story in greater detail, experience empathy and support for the pain the story reveals, and understand the story of the trauma pain (Ell, 1996). Telling the story of trauma pain allows others to help the client continue the story while changing the story line in a way that results in a more functional ending for the client (Bell, 1995). Both play and art can be utilized with traumatized children and their parents to help them actualize the healing dynamic of telling in a more effective, in-depth manner (Bell, 1995; Gil, 1991; Moon, 1990; Tick, 2001).

CHINESE CHECKERS WITH THE JAMES FAMILY

Mr. and Mrs. James and their seven-year-old daughter, Jenny, were referred to a practitioner six months after they experienced an auto accident in which their fifteen-year-old son (Jenny's older brother) had been killed. The parents reported that they were all having trouble mourning the death of John, but that Jenny had "just gone blank" after the accident and had not yet been able to talk about her feelings. After a warm-up and relationship-building (i.e., holding) interview, the practitioner used the "marbles test procedure" (Lantz, 2000) to help the family talk about their trauma.

In the second family session, the practitioner presented the family with a traditional six-pointed Chinese checkerboard, ten red marbles, ten yellow marbles, ten green marbles, and ten black marbles. Each family member was asked to choose a marble color (other than black) and then to make something artistic and beautiful as a family with the marbles and checkerboard. Each family member took a turn and placed one of their marbles on the board to make a design. The black marble was identified as John's color out of both respect and sorrow, and each family member also had to take turns placing a black marble in the design that they were making in honor of John. Mrs. James started crying as soon as she realized what the black marble represented. Mr. James started crying after he placed two marbles on the board, and Jenny started sobbing when she placed her first black marble on the board. Both Jenny and her parents then used the design session to talk about how much they missed John, about their sorrow and anger at God for taking John away, and about how hard it had been to cry and mourn. The marbles test procedure and the use of the black marbles helped the family members tell each other and the practitioner about their pain and facilitate the mourning process. It provided them with a helpful means of both displacing their feelings onto the checkerboard and seeing the pain outside themselves in a way that could be shared.

PLAY, ART, AND MASTERING

Mastering is the third dynamic in short-term existential intervention with children and their parents (Lantz & Raiz, 2003). After the family members are able to hold and tell their trauma pain, they must begin to find ways to process and master the pain (DeJong, 2002; Lantz & Gyamerah, 2002). That is, they must become able to control and channel the pain so that it does not dominate their lives, and they can begin to actually use the pain in constructive ways. Play and art can often be used with both parents and children to help them gain a sense of mastery over their suffering (Gil, 1991; Lantz, 2002; Moon, 1990; Tick, 2001).

THE BURKHART FAMILY'S DRAWINGS

The Burkharts were an African American family that consisted of the mother (Jean), the father (Jack), nine-year-old son (Sam), and a sixteen-year-old daughter (Ruth). The family was referred for intervention after they had been robbed at gunpoint while on vacation in a large city on the Atlantic coast. Since this event the son had started wetting his pants, the daughter was having nightmares, Mrs. Burkhart was having problems sleeping, and Mr. Burkhart was having trouble eating and going to work.

In the third family session the practitioner asked each family member to draw a picture of a rainbow that went over a black cloud (which represented the robbery) and ended at a treasure chest that contained information about what the family needed to do to get back to normal. Each family member was then asked to draw the contents of the treasure chest to find out what they needed to do. Mrs. Burkhart's drawing indicated that she needed sleeping pills, Mr. Burkhart's drawing indicated that he needed to start eating better, and both the son and the daughter's drawings indicated that they needed to learn to fight. After seeing the children's drawings, the father and the mother both agreed that learning to fight might be a good idea for the entire family.

At this point the practitioner directly told the father that he and his family had done the best thing they could have done by not fighting the robber and by giving the robber their money. The practitioner shared his belief that not fighting in that situation probably saved their lives. He then told the family that learning to fight might now be a good way to get over feeling so much anxiety. He agreed to help the family arrange for lessons at a martial arts studio that was both family friendly and near their home. The family continued to see the practitioner over a period of several weeks, and after the termination they continued to study karate as a family. All four family members were free of symptoms and made a good adjustment after their trauma experience. The family had used art to help them discover what Figley (1989) calls a healing theory to master their trauma pain. Their healing theory was to learn to fight.

PLAY, ART, AND HONORING

Honoring trauma pain refers to the healing process of identifying and making use of the meaning potentials embedded in the problem occurrence (Frankl, 1969; Lantz, 2002). Honoring the trauma involves becoming aware of opportunities for giving to the world that are suggested by the memory of the trauma (Lantz & Gyamerah, 2002). Honoring helps the traumatized child and family fill an existential meaning vacuum that may develop after an experience of emotional suffering. Honoring can sometimes be facilitated through the use of play and art (Gil, 1981).

BUILDING BLOCKS AND THE GREEN FAMILY

The Green family was referred for intervention by their pediatrician after their nine-year-old daughter stopped talking. The daughter (June) had stopped talking shortly after her next-door neighbor and best friend, Mary (ten years old) died of leukemia. Although Mr. and Mrs. Green felt they had done a good job preparing their daughter for Mary's death, they were upset that "apparently we didn't do enough." The practitioner met with the family six times over several months, and they made excellent progress. June's grades improved, she started talking again, and the parents became more at ease with their own functioning, as well as the family's. Described below is one intervention that seemed particularly helpful to the family's honoring of Mary.

The activity of using blocks to build towers "toward heaven" is a play therapy method for getting children to reflect on spiritual issues. This connects them with a universal "heaven-seeking" theme that is also reflected in the fact that most worship centers have towers and steeples that reach toward heaven (Tick, 2001). Toward the end of the intervention, the practitioner gathered a set of wooden blocks and asked the Green family to try to build a tower of blocks reaching high up in the air toward heaven and to see how high they could get. June laughed and said she would use the tower to look for Mary. She then shared that when she stopped talking, she had also stopped praying. June decided that she needed to pray again to make sure Mary was okay and still in heaven. Shortly after the tower blocks interview, June started volunteering two hours a week at the Leukemia Society office to fulfill her school's community service requirement and to honor her friend Mary.

SUMMARY

Short-term existential intervention with children and their parents involves the elements of holding, telling, mastering, and honoring trauma pain. This chapter outlined and illustrated the use of play and art to facilitate the process of intervention with traumatized children and their parents. Play and art can be therapeutic because the types of communication that occur with those modalities match the language of childhood. Intervention is thus effective when the practitioner can help the family utilize that language to help children learn and grow.

The four previous clinical illustrations were provided to give the reader specific ideas about how play and art can facilitate each of the four elements of short-term existential intervention. The chapter concludes with an illustration of the total process of intervention with another family.

BILLY'S BEHAVIORAL PROBLEMS

Billy Brown was a four-year-five-month-old African American child referred for intervention with his parents after being sexually abused by a teacher at his day-care center. This teacher was found guilty of molesting three young male students. After Billy was molested, he became difficult to manage at home and started having bad dreams at night that scared him. His parents reported that he was having more and more outbursts and had become extremely avoidant of all male adults except for his father.

Billy came to his first appointment holding his parents' hands, not talking, and looking apprehensive. He seemed to not hear the practitioner's questions and ignored all friendly overtures. In order to engage Billy, the practitioner got out crayons and paper and had each parent draw a tree. Billy was given the same materials but was told that he might or might not want to draw a tree. After his parents each drew several trees, Billy joined in and started drawing trees and also birds, his dog, his home, and (with encouragement) his day-care center. After that first meeting the practitioner met with the parents without Billy so that he could more fully assess Billy's emotional status. Mrs. Brown was afraid that Billy might be scarred for life, and Mr. Brown didn't know what to think. It was decided with the practitioner's encouragement that the best resource for Billy would be family intervention using play and art as the agents of change. The parents agreed to come to play therapy two times a week for at least five weeks and then see where things stood.

In the third family meeting, Billy continued his pattern of avoiding the practitioner's efforts to connect with him. Billy actively rejected the therapist's drawings, which were offered to him in an attempt to enter the themes of Billy's play and art. Billy started tearing up the practitioner's drawings, which the practitioner interpreted as "Billy doing a good job practicing staying away from strangers and getting mad when they don't leave him alone." After this, the practitioner started rapidly drawing pictures of adult men and gave them to Billy, who crumpled them up and threw them away. After twenty minutes, the practitioner and Billy's father began making a Lincoln Logs jail, which, they explained, the "police use to lock up bad guys." Billy started drawing pictures of "bad guys" he hoped would be sent to jail and then crumpled them up and put them in the Lincoln Logs jail.

During the next few weeks, the practitioner utilized art and play to help Billy tell his parents how mad he was at the bad guy who had hurt him. Billy used paper, crayons, and clay to make representations of a bad guy, which Billy could either destroy or put in the Lincoln Logs jail. Billy enjoyed making bad guy figures out of clay, smashing them with his fist, and then putting them in the Lincoln Logs jail.

Starting in the fourth week of intervention, the practitioner told Billy and his parents that it was the job of the police to put bad guys in jail and that it was the family's job to learn to stay away from people they thought might be bad guys. The practitioner asked Billy to make a plastic fence model corral for a plastic horse figurine. Billy was also invited to make a gate so that good guys could feed or water or play with the horse, but the bad guys would be kept out. Billy made a swinging fence gate that he could use to control who he let in to see the horse and who he kept out. Over the next five sessions, Billy and his parents practiced deciding who could visit the horse and who could not. The practitioner presented them with a variety of toy figurines who wanted to visit the horse. Billy and his parents practiced saying yes or no to a wide variety of symbolic toy visits, including Batman, Mickey Mouse, the Lion King, Donald Duck, the wolf from Little Red Riding Hood, the Seven Dwarfs, Snow White, Fat Albert, Santa Claus, Peter Pan, the Straw Man, Darth Vader, and Captain Hook. Toward the end of this play theme, Billy decided he was ready to go back to day care since the bad guy had been put in jail.

The practitioner and family continued with this intervention for two weeks beyond the original five-week intervention contract. In the last stage of intervention the number of sessions was gradually reduced to one per month. At termination Billy was free of bad dreams and outbursts, and he was selectively able to relate to appropriate older males. The family returned for two additional sessions six months after termination, when Mrs. Brown discovered she was pregnant and Billy learned he was to become an older brother. Although Billy was initially upset about this development, he resolved it by deciding that he could protect his little sister or brother from bad guys and show her or him how to protect horses.

9

Dream Work

DREAMS ARE FORMS OF THINKING THAT OCCUR WHEN THERE IS A MIN-
imal level of brain activation, external stimuli have limited entry into the mind, and
the self system (the "I" or the "me") is shut down. Dreams are something that we experience because the thinking is very real and makes use of our sight and hearing.
We are usually the main actor, and our dreams can be very emotional.

Many theorists have addressed the therapeutic potential of dream analysis,
since dream content seems to touch on activities and themes in our lives. Sigmund
Freud (1917) believed that the manifest, or surface, content of dreams is symbolic,
and that the deeper meaning of dreams is their depiction of what we fantasize about
and wish for. Alfred Adler held that dreams were an open pathway to our truest
thoughts, emotions, and actions (Ansbacher & Ansbacher, 1956). He wrote that
dreams are a way of overcompensating for the shortcomings in our waking lives.
Carl Jung (1968) claimed that the function of dreams is to compensate for those
parts of the psyche (total personality) that are underdeveloped in waking life. Fritz
Perls (1978) believed that dreams are projections of disowned parts of our person-
alities, and that the main technique of therapy is to focus on what the client is reluctant to face in real life. Cognitive psychologist Calvin Hall (1953) wrote that
dreams represent a process of generating ideas by translating concepts into images.
For him, dream interpretation consists of the reverse process of translating images
into their referent ideas. While there is much uncertainly about the nature of
dreams, it is widely accepted that they may be revealing of what is on a person's
mind.

In short-term existential intervention, dream reflection is a process of dialogue
between the client (as dreamer) and the practitioner (Lantz, 1992). The practitioner's function is not to tell the client what a dream means, nor to formulate for
the client the unconscious material that may be embedded in the dream. The practitioner's function in dream reflection should be Socratic in that he or she demonstrates interest, curiosity, and concern and uses questions to help the client focus
on clues in the dream that might help him or her become more aware of forgotten
meanings, repressed meaning potentials, solutions, and strengths (Lantz, 1997).

Dream reflection is best done after the client and practitioner have developed a
positive treatment alliance. Talking about dreams may feel initially awkward to a

client, so he or she may not be comfortable exploring dream content until there is trust that the practitioner will respect such an activity. The positive relationship allows the practitioner to help the client use dream reflection to *notice* meaning potentials in the future, *actualize* and make use of such meaning potentials in the here and now, and *re-collect* and honor meanings previously actualized but deposited in the past. The following case vignettes are examples of how dream reflection can be used in short-term existential intervention.

NOTICING IN BILL'S DREAM

Bill was an Appalachian male who presented the following dream in his fourth session with the practitioner:

I was working with a bunch of men in a coal mine. The men dropped me off at the ninth level and I went down a long tunnel toward a wall of coal. My job was to dig out the coal, so I used my pick ax and started to dig. After a few minutes of digging I heard a voice from behind the wall of coal. I got scared, and then I woke up. I've had this dream about four or five times, and I always wake up when I hear the voice. It's a very scary dream.

The following dialogue occurred after Bill presented his dream. The dialogue was recorded on audiotape but has been modified for purposes of brevity and confidentiality.

Practitioner (P): Who were the men who left you off on the ninth level? Did you know them? Did you recognize them?

Client (C): No, I didn't know them.

P: Do you have any feeling about who they might be?

C: Well, they were from my hometown. It's a coal town, you know. I don't know . . . maybe my uncles. Yea, probably my uncles. That feels right.

P: How about the ninth level? What's that about? Any ideas? (The therapist knows that Bill's father died when Bill was nine years old.)
(Long silence)

P: Any ideas at all?

C: No . . . No, not really.
(Silence)

P: OK, so let's go back to the coal wall. What does being next to a coal wall mean? What could it mean? Who was the voice? Who comes into mind?

C: It just now popped into my mind. It's probably my father. He died in a coal mine accident. He died when I was nine. In some ways I've been hoping to hear his voice ever since.

P: So, is there any chance that getting dropped off on level nine speaks to this?

C: (Starting to cry) Hell, yes! That's it! Level nine, and I lost him when I was nine . . . God, that's clear!
(Client cries.)

P: So look . . . these men who dropped you off . . . may be your uncles. Did any of your uncles take you up and give you time after your dad died? Did any of them help you out?

C: Hell, no! . . . Hell, no! I was on my own. . . . They helped Mom out with money and stuff until she could get a job and start working. But hell, no! My mom started working, and my uncles didn't spend time with me at all. Hell, no!

P: So this does not sit well with you. . . . They left you off at level nine. No father, and they left you off to "pick" for yourself. (Long silence)

C: God, yes . . . shit. I bet it's my father behind the wall. I bet it's his voice. (Long silence)

P: Maybe yes . . . maybe no. Who else could it be? Who else might it be?

C: Hell, I don't know . . . nobody. It's got to be my father.

P: Is there anyone else you know who has lost a father? Anyone else you think it might be? (Client starts to cry again.)

C: Shit! It's my kids behind the wall. You're right. It was a child's voice! God . . . I'm a workaholic and I don't spend time with my kids. Damn . . . I'm doing the same thing to them that happened to me. Shit! (Client cries.)

P: Pretty good dream . . . real good dream . . . a tough-talking dream.

C: Yeah . . . Hell of a dream. I'm becoming a dead man to my kids. I put them behind a wall. . . . God, I've got to turn this around.

P: So the meaning potential in the dream is about not being a dead man—a dead father to your kids, and the thing you need to do is . . . ?

C: Spend time with them . . . stop being a workaholic! Start being a father!

P: Start being a father. Maybe take the opportunity your father never got. Do what your dad didn't get to learn to do.

C: (Crying) Yeah! That's it. It's a good dream . . . a tough dream! Shit . . . shit!

NOTICING IN BETH'S DREAM

Beth was an African American woman who requested intervention after she lost her job. She felt depressed, experienced anxiety attacks, and wanted to stop drinking. Beth initially had great difficulty talking during her intervention sessions, so she and the practitioner used art and art reflection to help her talk. Beth stopped drinking during the initial stage of intervention and reported that using painting and doing art provided her with great relief. She continued to use art and art reflection throughout treatment but would occasionally bring a dream to her sessions for discussion, such as the following:

I was walking down a street in my old neighborhood, and I went past some of my parents' friends. They all hung their heads and wouldn't look at me except for Mr. Jacks. Old man Jacks was always nice to me. He was my dad's best friend and I liked him. Well . . . old man Jacks told me that they were going to dinner but I couldn't come with them cause I wasn't clean. He told me I had to get clean before I could go to the table. I felt sad but I didn't argue.

After considerable talk and reflection about the dream, Beth decided that old man Jacks was not being mean but wanted her to go back to church and to confession and then take communion. In that way Beth could go to the table at her neighborhood Catholic Church. Beth felt the dream was telling her that she was not clean because she had had an abortion after she was raped in her last year of high school. Beth believed that she was a baby killer. She felt that old man Jacks wanted her to go back to church and that he was on my side. Beth felt that since old man Jacks wanted her to go back to church, that probably meant it was time. After this dream, Beth was able to notice her religious values and meanings and return to her home parish. She went to confession and then took communion for the first time since she had been raped. For Beth, the meaning potential to be noticed in her dream was to go back to church and receive forgiveness from her priest, God, her parents, community, and herself.

NOTICING IN SAM'S DREAM

Sam requested intervention because he was feeling depressed and was experiencing confusion about his life. He was a fifty-five-year-old widower who was proud to have raised two wonderful children who had both graduated from college. Sam worked as a comptroller in a company he had started, developed, and eventually sold five years ago. He was financially independent and could retire anytime. Sam reported that he was tired of work and had been thinking of retirement, but didn't know what to do if he did retire. Sam reported the following dream in his fourth session:

I was walking to work and needed to get there by nine. When I came to Main Street, I turned left instead of going straight. But I get to my office by going straight! I couldn't figure out why I turned left. The only thing that was on the left was my church, but it wasn't Sunday. There was no good reason for turning left. When I woke up I felt happy.

Sam and the practitioner spent a great deal of time reflecting on this dream. Both believed that turning left in the dream was important, and the therapist told Sam that he needed to find out what's in that direction. After noticing that turning left would take him to his church, Sam reported that when he had been a young man, he wanted to go to a seminary and become a minister. Sam reported that he had given that up after he married and had kids. Sam decided that going left on Main Street was telling him that he should return to his old goal of enrolling in seminary school now that he had the time and money.

Sam did retire, and eventually he went to study theology at a seminary school. He got to study the material that he didn't have a chance to study when he was a young man. To Sam, the meaning potential discovered in his dream was turning left and returning to school after all those years. Sam reported that his depression left him after his Main Street dream. Sam moved out of the city to a small, rural town and became a deacon at a small Episcopal church.

RE-COLLECTING IN ELEANOR'S DREAM

The previous examples illustrate the use of the dream to help clients notice meaning potentials in their lives. The following material illustrates the use of dream reflection to help an older Appalachian client to re-collect, and honor meanings actualized previously but deposited in the past.

Eleanor was referred for intervention by one of the nurses at her nursing home who had attended a workshop where a presentation was given on honoring and reminiscence therapy. The nurse believed that Eleanor could use some help in that way. Eleanor agreed that she felt sad most of the time and would be happy to have someone to talk with. She responded extremely well to intervention (most likely because she was receiving special attention from another person on a regular basis), and her symptoms of depression rapidly lifted. After a few weeks of intervention, Eleanor started using her sessions to remember, re-collect, and honor the meanings she had previously actualized. During her fifth treatment session, she presented the following dream:

I was in a canoe with Betty, and we were floating down Sundy Creek. It was summer. Betty was my best friend when I was young. We went to grade school and high school together. We both loved to swim and hike and to float down the creek in that old canoe we had. We were laughing and probably talking about boys. That's the dream. Just me and Betty floating down Sundy Creek.

The following dialogue is presented from memory. It is not perfectly accurate, but both Eleanor and the practitioner reviewed it and believe it to be essentially true.

Practitioner (P): Sundy Creek. So you grew up in Athens County. Is that right?

Client (C): How did you know that?

P: My family is from Jacksonville and I know the area. So were you from Glouster, or Chauncy, or Jacksonville? Which one?

C: (Laughing) None of them. I was from Shawnee. We would go to Glouster and put the canoe in there, and my father would drive downstream to Chauncy and pick us up there later in the day. It was nice.

P: I know Shawnee. My great uncle was from there. . . . His name was John Lantz. . . . Did you know him?

C: Oh my goodness. . . . You are one of them Shawnee Lantzes. (Laughing) You always seemed so nice. You can't be related to them. (Laughing)

P: I'm afraid so. My family moved away . . . to get away from coal mining. Lots of them moved to Columbus. Even some of the ones from Shawnee.

C: My goodness . . . you know about my hometown.

P: So when did you move to Columbus?

C: When I got married. We moved so we could go to college. And then we had kids. But I still loved my hometown!

P: Do you ever go back?

C: Not for years and years.

P: What happened to Betty?

C: (Starting to cry) She died about ten years ago. She lived here at this nursing home for a while. I still miss her.

P: So tell me more about you and Betty and Shawnee and growing up in Southeast Ohio. Go ahead . . . I really would like to hear.

At this point Eleanor initiated the process of re-collection. Over the next few weeks, she told the practitioner many wonderful stories about growing up in southeast Ohio, about moving to Columbus, about raising her kids, and about work and friends. Eleanor enjoyed recollection but felt guilty about ruminating on the past. She had apparently been told by some of the nurses at her nursing home that ruminating on the past was a bad thing.

The following dialogue re-creates how the practitioner helped Eleanor to understand that reminiscence and re-collection are not bad. The practitioner's comments are based upon Frankl's (1969) belief that remembering, recollecting, and honoring meanings deposited in the past are a useful way to shrink an existential vacuum in the present.

Client (C): This was a wonderful meeting. I enjoyed talking about these things so much . . . even though it's bad.

Practitioner (P): Bad? . . . Bad? . . . How so?

C: Well, the nurses tell me I shouldn't spend so much time in the past. That it's bad for me.

P: Really? I don't agree with that! I think they're wrong. I really do!

C: Why? . . . Please tell me!

P: The things you told me about today are real. You did them. You and Betty and your father and your family, you did them. And you put these things into the past. You made them forever real. It's like you put them in a bank. They are yours, and you have every right to take them out and remember them and look at them and enjoy them again. That's your right, because you did these things! You made them real, and when you remember them, it's like you are honoring them. I really don't think that the nurses understand this. I think it's good for you to remember and be proud of the memories you made. I like the canoe memory best . . . just floating down Sundy Creek. That's a good one. . . . I want to hear more!

C: (Crying) Oh . . . that makes sense. Thank you . . . thank you so much.

ACTUALIZING IN JOYCE'S DREAM

In this final vignette, the practitioner and client use dream reflection to facilitate understanding and awareness of patterns that have disrupted the client's ability to actualize and make use of the meaning potentials in her life. In her fourth session, Joyce shared the following dream:

I was in a taxi cab. I was going to a job interview. When we got to the office building where I was to be interviewed, I tried to open the cab door, but it would not open. I asked the man who was driving the taxi to help, but he told me that he wouldn't help. So . . . I didn't get the job.

After considerable reflection, Joyce decided that the dream outlined her long-term pattern of trying to get other people to "do things for me." Joyce reported that she was especially good at getting men to "take care of me" and that she was disappointed because the practitioner was not overly eager to "solve all my problems." Joyce decided that her dream gave her permission to tell the practitioner about her methods of getting by that she might use in therapy. Joyce and the practitioner were able to use this dream to reflect upon their relationship and Joyce's consistent and repetitive dependency patterns and to develop an intervention contract outlining what was Joyce's job and what was the practitioner's job. The dream helped the practitioner to point out the dependency patterns Joyce used to disrupt her ability to actualize the meaning potentials in her life and to resolve crisis.

SUMMARY

The nature, purpose, and objective function of dreams are not known, although numerous theories have been proposed. Still, dream reflection can be an effective element of the existential intervention process. It can be used by the practitioner and client to consider symbolic material helps the client notice meaning potentials in the future, re-collect and honor meanings previously actualized but deposited in the past, and better understand functioning patterns used to actualize or disrupt meaning potentials in his or her life.

10

Life Stage Crisis Interventions

THE *LIFE STAGE* CRISIS IS THE MOST FREQUENTLY OCCURRING CRISIS EX-
perience in people's lives. Freud (1917), Erickson (1959), Haley (1976), and Carter
and McGoldrick (2005) are well-known theorists who consider the life stage crisis
to be the most common as well as the most frequently occurring opportunity for
people to experience positive change. Erickson (1959) believed that significant
changes in social functioning can occur when we move from one stage to another
in the human life cycle. He wrote about the stages of infancy, early childhood, play
age, school age, adolescence, young adulthood, adulthood, and mature age, along
with the unique challenges that we face at those transition times. Haley (1976) described the period of life stage transition as the time when we are most open to
change. Lantz (1978, 1993, 2000) has written about the opportunities for change
that exist during transition periods in the family life cycle.

This chapter provides a basic overview of the meanings and meaning potentials
that occur in life cycle changes and describes some existential intervention opportunities to be found during these changes. With a few exceptions (such as Sheridan,
2003), most developmental theorists have ignored existential aspects of life cycle
transitions.

Life cycle and other developmental theories have fallen out of favor among
many human service theorists and practitioners in recent years (Hutchison, 2007).
This is because stage theories tend to see all people as proceeding through the same
cycle. With increased awareness of human diversity within and among societies, it
is now more fully appreciated that there is great variability in human experience
from a developmental perspective. Existential practitioners need to organize their
assessments and intervention decisions around certain relevant variables in clients'
lives. Not all people experience the same transitional challenges at the same times
in their lives, but all people do experience life transitions within the context of their
social group and culture. The existential practitioner must be able to understand
each client's unique life context in order to assess the nature and impact of these
transitions.

In a family life cycle model, human developmental progression is understood
to include two components: individual growth and development tasks, and family
network acceptance and encouragement tasks (Lantz, 1993, 2000; Lantz & Ahern,
1994). From this perspective a person's physical, psychological, social, and spiritual

development can be significantly enhanced or disrupted by the family, depending on the extent of the family's readiness to accept and reinforce individual developmental progression, and to move into the family life-cycle stage that will most encourage growth for all members (Berg & Dolan, 2001).

THE HUMAN LIFE CYCLE

The concept of a life cycle incorporates the following three understandings (Ell, 1996):

1. Both families and individuals go through a series of life cycle stages.
2. The life cycle includes both individual developmental tasks and family-acceptance and encouragement tasks.
3. The life cycle includes individual and family progression on a physical, psychosocial, and meaning-spiritual level.

Although many life cycle models have been presented in the human services literature, the model of Carter and McGoldrick (2005) is used here. This model is well known in the social work literature, and it lends itself to a holistic understanding of human and family development. This family life-cycle model includes several developmental stages, including those of the unmarried or unattached young person, the young couple, the couple or parent with young child, the family unit including an adolescent, the launching of children, and the later adult. The model's major limitation is that it is not as useful in understanding couples who decide not to have children. Each stage is considered separately.

THE UNMARRIED OR UNATTACHED YOUNG ADULT

When young people leave their families to live on their own, they are both signifying and practicing their ability to live and function with their own values, meanings, and spiritual beliefs. They are also practicing their ability to live without the consistent support, encouragement, direction, and control that may have been present within their families of origin. In this stage of the family life cycle, a young adult experiments with new values, spiritual beliefs, and meaning opportunities that may be different from the patterns of meaning actualization taught by their parents or parent figures (Lantz, 2000). In the young adult stage, people must discover the strengths of their own values and meanings and of their own special ways of discovering and making use of meaning potentials. In many instances, a mentoring approach to crisis intervention can be extremely helpful, as the following case illustrates.

OFF TO COLLEGE

Michael Adams, an eighteen-year-old college freshman, had been at the head of his high-school class academically. At the end of his first semester in college, however, he

developed symptoms of severe depression, including crying spells, suicidal thoughts, social isolation, confusion, and a sleep disturbance, when he received only average grades
(a C-plus average). Each of Michael's five intervention sessions revolved around his developing insights into how, in the past, he had used his intellect and superior academic
performance to help him feel meaningful. Michael and the practitioner attempted to discover additional ways that the client could experience a meaningful personal identity.
They were able to work toward these goals through a series of discussions about the client's values and emerging priorities. Michael learned to see value in other activities be-
sides academics, and he became more successful in making friends, expanding his range
of leisure interests, dating, and eventually improving his grades. During intervention
Michael learned that he was more than just a brain, and he expanded his skills for discovering meaning, especially in the area of social relationships.

A second task of the young unmarried adult is courtship and falling in love.
These activities, when successful, may lead to new emotional commitments, exclusive partnerships, or marriage. It is well known that many young partnerships and
marriages fail because the partners have yet to learn how to overcome a narcissistic concern for just the self and that successful partnering has something to do with
adoration of the significant other. For many young people a significant spiritual task
is courtship and learning how to fall in love with an individual and the world beyond
the self. Becoming committed to something outside the self is difficult and also
risky, given that the chances of loss or disappointment are very real. At times intervention can be done in the form of premarital therapy or relationship counseling,
which can help people move from the stage of narcissistic self-concern to a more
adult stage of caring for significant others (Golan, 1978).

THE YOUNG COUPLE

In the young couple stage of the family life cycle, two people must learn to move
beyond courtship and adoration to a pattern of consistent giving, loving, and self-
transcendent concern for the significant other as the basis for meaning awareness.
In this stage a young couple learns that love is both adoration and hard work and
that sharing, commitment, integrity, and consistent effort are as important in a successful partnership as romantic love. The individuals in the relationship learn to discover and experience meanings in commitment, in the art of pleasuring the significant other, and with the responsibilities that go along with being a loving and
caring partner. The individuals learn to experience meaningful identity as both an
adored individual and a hard-working member of a loving, two-person family group.
Intervention can often be a useful aid to a young couple that can help them start to
learn to do the hard work that must occur in a successful and meaning-filled marriage or partnership (Berg & Dolan, 2001).

THE AMBIVALENT COUPLE

Stan and Mark were gay men who recently moved into an apartment together. They were close friends and had sexual relations occasionally, but neither had made a commitment to the other, and each had a separate social life. Their relationship came to a crisis point when Stan demanded that Mark make an exclusive commitment to him or end the relationship entirely. Mark was ambivalent about that point but agreed to several sessions of counseling with Stan to try to resolve the issue.

In a series of discussions over four sessions, the practitioner helped both men to elaborate on what they wanted in this relationship, and in an ideal relationship. He was able to help Mark, and Stan to a lesser degree, see that his ideal relationship did not involve much of a need for compromise and did not recognize conflict as an ongoing reality. In short, Mark was still rather self-absorbed in his belief that relationships were about getting his own needs met and helping the other person to do the same, but only if it did not require compromise. The practitioner raised the themes of work, sacrifice, and pain as relationship realities and helped the couple describe how these themes had become apparent in their interactions since they moved in together. They both viewed these exercises as constructive, although as an outcome they separated, as Mark became aware that he was not yet ready for such a commitment. Stan and Mark remained friends.

THE YOUNG-CHILD FAMILY

The arrival of a child forces a couple to develop a new set of skills involved in reaction to the new meaning potentials and meaning opportunities to be found in raising a child. It is a bit of a surprise for the couple to discover that, just as they are learning to do a good job living and loving in a two-person group, they must drop their two-person self-transcendence skills and learn to be a three-person group. In many instances an existential practitioner can help the parents learn to adore the child without either hurting the feelings of the spouse or abandoning the spouse. The practitioner can be useful in helping the parents learn to give to and love the young child in spite of the fact that such love is often returned through the presentation of dirty diapers, spit-up milk, and other such "gifts." The practitioner can coach the new parents on how to actualize the meaning potentials to be found in bathing a child, rocking and feeding it, and losing a great deal of sleep in its honor. In the young child stage of the family life cycle, family members learn to discover and experience meaning through the experiences of additional closeness, intimacy, and nurturance that are triggered by the existence of a child (Berg & Dolan, 2001; Lantz, 1993, 2000).

A major problem that sometimes occurs in this stage of the cycle is that parents do not learn to share the child, or they use the child to cement and symbolize their own parental and marital relationship. In such a situation, family-centered intervention is often the treatment of choice, as the following clinical material illustrates.

THE CHEATHAM FAMILY

Mrs. Cheatham was an African American mother who requested services for her seven-year-old son, who refused to go to school. When Mrs. Cheatham took her son to school he would become ill and vomit. The client wanted the practitioner to help her son face his problem. In the initial session, the practitioner discovered that Mr. and Mrs. Cheatham spent very little time together. Mr. Cheatham worked long hours and was involved in a number of community activities, leaving Mrs. Cheatham and their son by themselves for long periods of time. Mr. Cheatham enjoyed being away from home, as he viewed his wife as depressed and sad. This is an example of the vicious circle discussed in chapter 5, as Mrs. Cheatham's depression was made worse by Mr. Cheatham's absence, and his absences became more prolonged as he noticed her worsening depression.

Mrs. Cheatham stated that she wanted her son to go to school but admitted that she hated to face the day without his company. In this clinical situation, the son's school attendance problem signaled a disruption of meaning actualization in the parents' marital relationship. The son started attending school as Mr. and Mrs. Cheatham began to work seriously on rediscovering meaning in their marriage. They did this with the practitioner's help by learning the meaning of each other's moods, and deciding how they might more equitably share responsibility for the son. The practitioner suggested a variety of tasks for the couple to address between their meetings, all of which involved their spending more time together and talking together in new ways.

THE ADOLESCENT-STAGE FAMILY

In the adolescent stage of the family life cycle, parents and the adolescent child work on discovering and experiencing meaning through both closeness-intimacy and separation-autonomy (Walsh, 2003). Both parents and the adolescent must work on ambivalent feelings about closeness and separation. During this period an adolescent will quickly swing back and forth between wanting encouragement for independence and then wanting to be close for purposes of emotional support. The total family unit is in a constant state of flux, as family members move from these two poles of support and nurturance to autonomy and separation. They often will not know whether they are coming or going emotionally. In this situation, the family's primary goal is to let go in a way that fosters the adolescent's opportunities to practice autonomy and separation, while holding on in a way that provides nurturance without disturbing the adolescent's attempts to find a separate identity (Lantz, 2000).

THE FIRE SETTER

Carolyn, a fifteen-year-old white adolescent, was referred to a practitioner at a mental health center for an assessment after getting caught with several friends setting a fire to dry brush along the side of a highway. No one had been hurt, but the blaze was large, and it took several hours for the fire department to extinguish it. Carolyn faced legal charges for this incident and was being considered for possible incarceration by the juvenile court. Her mother had also become concerned that Carolyn was engaging in promiscuous sex.

Carolyn was the third and youngest child born to a middle-class couple; she had two brothers. Her parents complained that "she has no reason to behave as she does—she always had everything she needed." Still, Carolyn had frequently been in trouble with her parents, teachers, and other authority figures, tending to be argumentative, moody, and oppositional. Her father said, "She's an angry, unhappy, ungrateful kid." On the other hand, Carolyn was athletic and energetic and had excellent social skills. She had many friends, although many of them shared her negative attitudes and were considered by her parents to be poor influences. Carolyn had average intelligence but did poorly in school, with no evident motivation to study.

In conducting the assessment, the practitioner learned that Carolyn's parents (both fifty years old) had been married for thirty years. They reported that the marriage was stable and that they had tried to raise Carolyn to be a responsible person. Her mother in particular felt that she had spent more time with Carolyn than with her other two children, trying to help her develop appropriate values and interests. Carolyn was seven and nine years younger than her brothers. She had cordial relationships with them but, due to the age difference, they were not close. Carolyn expressed a different view of the relationship with her parents. She said her mother was overbearing and would never allow Carolyn out of her sight. She said that her father was okay but distant. She felt that he worked long hours and was not very involved in her life. Carolyn added that in her opinion, her dad was not very involved in her mother's life either.

The practitioner learned that Carolyn's upbringing was affected by a critical event. Her mother, who had wanted a daughter very badly, had given birth to a stillborn girl three years before Carolyn was born. This was a traumatic event for the family, and her mother was depressed for a year after the event. When she became pregnant with Carolyn, she was thrilled but apprehensive. She and her husband learned of the baby's gender early during the pregnancy, and she became completely focused on having a safe pregnancy and delivery. When Carolyn was born, her mother became a devoted but overprotective parent. In fact, her husband was angry about his wife's attitude and withdrew emotionally from her. The practitioner concluded that Carolyn was angry about the perceived overprotection.

As she got to know the client over time, the practitioner saw a pattern emerge in which Carolyn was afraid of getting close to or trusting anyone for fear of being consumed by them and of losing her identity completely. At the same time, Carolyn felt empty and abandoned by caregivers and friends who would not provide her with the security she needed. Carolyn did not have opportunities for age-appropriate movement toward independence because of her mother's well-meaning but intrusive presence. Through reflective discussion, the practitioner encouraged Carolyn to talk about the emotions she experienced in her current life activities, rather than project blame elsewhere. She helped Carolyn understand some of her relationship patterns and helped her grasp the issue of her ambivalence in relationships. The practitioner used their relationship to demonstrate how Carolyn tended to react to others when issues of intimacy emerged. She encouraged the client to explore some of her talents and interests, such as swimming and a school service club that allowed students to visit nursing homes.

The practitioner met with the client and her parents together several times. She pointed out the caring of the parents and educated them about the nature of Carolyn's interpersonal problems. The family was encouraged to talk more openly among themselves, and the parents were encouraged to support Carolyn's healthy activities. In short, corrective relationships might help Carolyn break her "approach–threat–anger–acting-out" cycle. With this understanding, her relationships began to improve and her acting-out behaviors decreased. She was not incarcerated for her criminal behaviors but instead received probation.

LAUNCHING CHILDREN

Launching children is the stage of the family life cycle in which parents or parent figures give children permission to leave the family unit. It is the stage in which they experience the empty-nest syndrome (Walsh, 2003). When both parents are still at home they often discover that they are not as close as they once were. There is often a meaning vacuum in the marriage since the parents no longer share daily concern for taking care of their children. In this situation, parents often need to move into a new courtship period and learn to adore each other again, if they are committed to the relationship. The following vignette illustrates intervention with a couple in the launching-of-children stage.

THE DERRINGERS

Mr. and Mrs. Derringer were referred for marital therapy by their attorney, whom they had initially consulted about divorce. They had decided to try marital therapy prior to making any final decisions about a divorce. The couple reported that they started having problems after their children left home; the son had gone to the army, and the daughter to college. The only real interest that they shared was their children, and now that the children were gone, they had no meaningful mutual interests. Intervention helped Mr. and Mrs. Derringer by giving them the opportunity to talk about and discover new meanings in their marriage that were not dependent upon their mutual concern for the children. The practitioner saw the couple five times, using the sessions to reflect back feeling content of what the spouses were communicating to each other. The Derringers became aware that they had trouble communicating their emotional needs because they were not even sure what those needs were after so many years of focusing on children. Through a series of exercises the practitioner helped the couple prioritize their needs (emotional, vocational, affectional, sexual, recreational, domestic, and spiritual) and discuss how they wanted those needs to be fulfilled. Through this process they developed a new affection for one another and began spending time with one another again. The couple decided to remain together.

THE LATER ADULT STAGE

In the later adult stage of the family life cycle, parents or parent figures who have succeeded in launching children often experience a period of harmony that lasts until one or both face retirement, health problems, or death. Facing such problems, aging family members often must find new methods of experiencing meaning that do not depend on the job, children, or the relationship with the spouse who has passed away (Lantz, 1993, 2000). The following example illustrates intervention with an older adult woman faced with the task of finding and actualizing new meaning opportunities.

THE VOLUNTEER

Mrs. Ebenger presented for intervention with crying spells, loss of energy, boredom, and the feeling that her life was empty. She reported that she had retired two years previously and that she could not adjust. Her husband had died fifteen years earlier and her children were grown and busy with their own families. Mrs. Ebenger was also worried about the monetary cost of the intervention. Although she described her income as adequate, she was not sure if she had "extra" income to pay for meetings with the practitioner. She reported that she spent most of her time watching television and puttering around her apartment. She had no hobbies and few friends and did not belong to any organizations or clubs.

The practitioner presented the client with an option that he felt might improve her life satisfaction. He arranged for weekly sessions with Mrs. Ebenger at a reduced cost, provided she work off the part of the cost she could not afford by volunteering at a local settlement house. Mrs. Ebenger came to six sessions and then stopped because "it interferes with my time with the kids and people at the settlement house." She reported that she felt better, had greater energy, and was no longer feeling bored and empty. From an existential perspective, Mrs. Ebenger felt better because the practitioner had helped her restore meaning in her life by arranging an opportunity for her to perform meaningful work at the settlement house.

SUMMARY

Developmental or stage theories of human development have fallen out of favor in recent decades as a greater interest in developmental diversity has emerged. Although all people and all families are unique, the theory of family life stages can be useful to the existential practitioner in providing a general context for understanding family functioning. The six stages of the family life cycle described in this chapter provide the practitioner with an excellent tool to identify both disruptions in human meaning awareness and opportunities for meaning and spiritual development in the context of family life.

11

Intervention with Migration Clients

MIGRATION, OR THE MOVEMENT ACROSS STATE, REGIONAL, OR NATIONAL boundaries for purposes of assuming a new residence, is a way of life for millions of people each year. Even those who tend to stay put are increasingly affected by the racial and cultural diversity that comes with migration. Each year, for example, approximately one million people enter the United States for the purpose of establishing permanent residence (Organization for Economic Cooperation and Development, 2005). In the United States, over 22 million domestic migrants changed their state of residence between 1995 and 2000 (U.S. Census Bureau, 2003).

Whatever the reasons for a person or family's migration, the process is stressful and requires a great deal of personal adjustment. For that reason, migration crisis is second only to life stage crises in frequency of occurrence (Harper & Lantz, 1996). A person or family may experience a migration crisis in reaction to moving from one country to another, but such a crisis can also occur in reaction to a move from one geographical location to another within the same country. The hallmark trauma of migration crisis is loss (Lantz, 1978; Yalom, 1980). In the process of migration, individuals, couples, and families lose their connections to family, kin, relatives, landmarks, history, and place.

Economic issues often stimulate migration, as the move is frequently reactive to poverty conditions. In this situation the migrating person or family leaves home to discover new employment opportunities, better opportunities for advancement, better educational opportunities, or better pay. At other times, migration is stimulated by political oppression in the migrating client's home country. Thousands of migrants to the United States from Central and South America, as well as from Southeast Asia, have fled from political oppression in their land of origin (Harper & Lantz, 1996).

ANOMIC DEPRESSION

Anomic depression often occurs in reaction to an individual or family's migration experience (Lantz, 1993, 2000). This type of depression is characterized by feelings of emptiness, low self-esteem, and discouragement that result from a disruption to the sense of meaning and purpose in life. Anomic depression occurs when the migration experience disrupts a client or family's ability to notice, actualize, and honor the meanings and meaning potentials in their lives.

Reactive anomic depression may be triggered by any of the following issues:

◆ The migration client's separation from traditional methods of religious worship
◆ The loss of contact with extended family, friends, kin, and clan
◆ Language difficulties that occur when the client moves into a new culture
◆ Separation from recreational and relaxation activities
◆ Experiences of oppression and discrimination in the new culture

Anomic depression is generally a crisis problem of adjustment rather than a manifestation of a client's internal deficiencies (Golan, 1978). It is a type of crisis triggered by a contextual event that disrupts meaning awareness. These reactive anomic problems can be overcome, however. They are often responsive to existential intervention techniques that can help clients reestablish a sense of meaning and purpose (Harper & Lantz, 1996). Linkage and advocacy activities on the part of the practitioner are also required to help the client establish new social and resource supports.

The existential practitioner must have a sound appreciation of cultural diversity in order to work effectively with persons who have experienced migration (see chapter 6 for a full discussion of this issue). More specifically, the practitioner must demonstrate either a curious or competent response to working with clients from other racial or cultural groups. What follows are a variety of clinical illustrations that serve as common examples of crisis, and crisis-reactive anomic depression, triggered by the experience of migration.

THE TAKASHIMA FAMILY

The Takashima family moved to central Ohio from Japan so that Mr. Takashima could continue his employment with a Japanese manufacturing company that was opening an assembly plant in the United States. Mr. Takashima was part of a group of Japanese managers picked by their company to plan and open the assembly plant. He spoke English but his wife and three children spoke only Japanese. Approximately three months after her arrival in the United States, Mrs. Takashima twisted and dislocated her oldest son's shoulder in a fit of rage while attempting to discipline him, and several days later she attempted suicide. Fortunately the suicide attempt failed, and Mrs. Takashima was admitted to a psychiatric hospital for a short stay. During her initial treatment sessions there she reported to the translator and staff that she was feeling empty and alone, and that her life had seemed meaningless since she had come to America. She reported that her husband worked twelve hours per day and that she was alone in a strange new country without friends, extended family, or support. She had not discovered a place to worship in her traditional manner, and she did not understand American ways. She reported that she attempted to end her life because she felt useless and without hope. Mr. Takashima reported that his wife had never exhibited symptoms of depression in the past and had never previously struck the children.

THE SARIANO FAMILY

Mr. and Mrs. Sariano came to the mental health center because Mrs. Sariano was upset and depressed and had been picking on their two young children. Upon questioning, this "picking" was more clearly described as "hitting and slapping." The Sariano family had originally moved from Puerto Rico to New York City and then had moved again to the Midwest. Mrs. Sariano reported that her children were getting on her nerves since she had moved to the Midwest. Mr. Sariano reported that his wife had never before hit their children. His wife stated that she could find no Spanish-speaking people in the new city and that she wanted to return to New York. She felt uncomfortable in church, as it was an Irish and Italian Catholic church. Mrs. Sariano reported that at times she had gotten help in New York from a spiritualist but that she could not find one in the new city. She reported feeling empty, as if her life were meaningless.

THE LIST FAMILY

The police brought Mr. List to a mental health center emergency unit after they responded to a domestic-dispute request for help. Mr. List was intoxicated and had hit his wife with his fist. Mrs. List reported that her husband had never hit her or any other family member in the past. She reported that Mr. List had been drinking heavily starting about three months after the family moved to the city from the mountains of eastern Tennessee. The family had moved to the Midwest because Mr. List's older sister had found him a factory job in the new city.

When Mr. List sobered up, he expressed considerable shame and guilt about his behavior. He reported that he had been feeling empty since he moved to the city. He reported that he felt strange and had problems making friends with the people at his job. He couldn't find "a church I feel good at," and he reported missing hunting, fishing, and roaming the woods. He reported that in spite of his new job and economic security, he still felt hollow.

THE BROWN FAMILY

Mrs. Brown came to the mental health center because she was depressed. She reported that she experienced crying spells and that her food tasted like cardboard. She was having problems sleeping and had lost ten pounds since she moved to the city from her rural hometown. She and her husband had moved to the big city from their small agricultural home community, she said, because Mr. Brown had found a good job and had a chance to go to college. The couple had a nine-month-old daughter, and Mrs. Brown stated that she was afraid she was not doing a good job as a mother since she had moved to the city. She said she was not neglecting her baby yet but was afraid she might do so. At times, she had to push herself to feed and clothe the child. She reported that back home her mother and older sister had given her much reassurance and support, and that when she moved, she lost them and all her favorite activities. She now felt very alone. She felt empty and that life was not as meaningful as it had been back home. She wanted help so that she would feel better and have more energy.

INDICATIONS OF REACTIVE ANOMIC DEPRESSION

The clients in the four clinical illustrations above described their anomic depression as a sense of emptiness and an inability to continue experiencing life as meaningful since migrating to a new geographical location. In each instance of anomic depression, the client family had been separated from the usual methods they had utilized back home in the past to symbolize and experience meaning. Each family had also experienced episodes of oppression and discrimination from members of the majority cultures in which they now lived, and this was creating additional major obstacles to finding life satisfaction.

INTERVENTION ACTIVITIES

In existential intervention with migrating clients, the practitioner uses a variety of intervention activities to facilitate the occurrence of the dynamics of holding, telling, mastering, and honoring. Three such treatment activities are network intervention, Socratic reflection, and social skills training (Harper & Lantz, 1996; Lantz, 1993). These activities are described here, and a clinical example is presented to illustrate their use.

Network Intervention

In most instances, anomic depression is reactive to a disruption in the migrating client's ability to utilize past relationships and activities for the purpose of meaning awareness. This disruption results from either a geographical change or a change in the client's cultural context in which old network meaning resources are no longer workable or available. Network intervention is used to increase the client's opportunities to establish or reestablish a sense of meaning through new social activities and relationships in the new cultural or geographical situation. Network intervention helps the client establish new relationships and activities that provide meaning opportunities that are compatible with the client's traditions, values, and past methods of discovering and realizing meaning. The clinical case management roles of linker, broker, advocate, and activist, discussed in chapter 2, are often used during network building. Through these processes the practitioner needs to have an awareness of formal and informal resources in the community with which to connect the migrating client. As a part of this environmental work the practitioner should always follow up with the client to make sure any linkages have been helpful. It is a mistake to assume that, for example, linking a Japanese wife with similar women in a new country will be successful merely because of their shared country of origin.

Socratic Reflection

In situations of reactive migration anomic depression, the client's potential meanings and meaning awareness have been repressed or denied (Frankl, 1969; Lantz, 1978). In *Socratic reflection,* the practitioner uses questions, comments, and interpretations and demonstrates personal interest to stimulate the client's reflection about the meaning opportunities and potentials that exist in his or her life. The major skill involved in Socratic reflection is the practitioner's ability to focus the client's thinking in areas where he or she will feel comfortable enough to consider and also be capable of considering new ways of addressing concerns related to anomic depression. Socratic reflection is most effective when the practitioner is aware of the importance of meaning perception and the seriousness of a disruption in the client's meaning awareness (Frankl, 1959; Lantz & Lantz, 2001).

Social Skills Training

The experience of cultural disruption demands that the client learn new problem-solving methods in the face of the disruption (Jilek, 1982). Learning a new language, new cultural norms, and new expectations in the new community, and even learning to eat new foods, are all important needs that are often underassessed and inadequately understood by many practitioners. In social skills training the practitioner teaches the migrating client new communication and problem-solving skills so that the client can make better use of the meaning opportunities that exist in the new community environment (Lantz, 1993, 2000). Offering the client such learning experiences through social skills training is a valuable mastering activity in instances of reactive anomic depression.

The following clinical illustration shows how the practitioner can utilize these three intervention strategies.

THE GRAHAM FAMILY

Mr. Graham was brought to the psychiatric hospital's emergency services unit by his cousin after overdosing on sleeping pills. Mr. Graham, age forty-two and married, reported that he tried to kill himself because he felt guilty that he had hurt his baby. He reported that he had lost his temper and spanked his two-year-old so hard that it left bruises. Mr. Graham reported, "I left home so I wouldn't do it again." After six days away from home, he went to a motel and overdosed on sleeping pills. He reported that he woke up a day later and called his cousin, who talked him into getting help at the hospital.

Mr. Graham said that he had been feeling depressed for about four months. He reported that he started feeling bad after he moved himself and his family to the city from his family home in West Virginia. He reported that he had never experienced such feelings at any time previously in his life. He had moved to the city for financial reasons after his cousin got him a factory job but reported having problems because "I miss being back home." Mr. Graham felt trapped because "there is no future back home" and because "I hate the city, where there is a future." The client reported that he wanted help, wanted to reunite with his wife and kids, and wanted to find a way to stay in the city "without getting crazy." He stated that he wouldn't go back to his family until he was sure that he could keep his temper under control.

Mr. Graham was first medically cleared by the hospital medical consultant and then was interviewed by an existential practitioner. The practitioner initially interviewed both Mr. Graham and his cousin and later in the day conducted a family interview with Mr. Graham, his wife, their sixteen-year-old daughter, and their two-year-old son. A caseworker from the local children's service protective agency also attended the last part of the family therapy interview. Based upon the assessment that the child abuse was a reaction to the family's migration situation, the child welfare caseworker decided not to open a formal case as long as the Graham family was receiving regular outpatient counseling. The caseworker and the Graham family agreed that the caseworker would drop in from time to time to see if the family was benefiting from treatment and ensure that no further incidents of abuse were occurring. Mrs. Graham, the cousin, and the sixteen-year-old daughter all confirmed Mr. Graham's report that he had no problems with drinking or depression prior to moving to the city and that he had never hit anyone in the family in the past.

Based on the family history and observations of family interaction during the conjoint family interview, the practitioner and consulting psychiatrist agreed that the Graham family was suffering with a reactive anomic depression. They agreed that the problems were reactive in nature and not the result of long-standing difficulties. The psychiatrist did not feel that anyone in the family could benefit much from antidepressant medication and agreed with the practitioner's plan to treat the Graham family on an outpatient basis using Socratic reflection, social skills training, and network intervention to help them reestablish a sense of meaning and purpose in their new city.

Table 11.1 outlines the intervention activities used with the Graham family to facilitate their resolution of the anomic depression crisis.

The Graham family received intervention for two months. The family members gradually learned to adjust to their new geographical and cultural situation in the city

Table 11.1. Treatment activities used with the Graham family

Socratic Reflection	Social Skills Training	Network Intervention
Scheduled weekly conjoint family treatment sessions using Socratic questions, interpretations, the therapist's interest and concern, and the family meaning history to help the family members recover and rediscover repressed family meanings that have been clouded by the stress of family migration	Scheduled weekly conjoint family treatment sessions to help the family members more effectively support each other and treat each other with meaning in spite of the stress of family migration	Connected the family to a number of supportive activities at the settlement house
	Arranged for the parents to join the Appalachian Club at the West Side Settlement House so that other Appalachian adults could coach the couple about surviving in the city	Connected the family with a fundamentalist church similar to the family's church back home
	Introduced the daughter to a seventeen-year-old peer counselor at the daughter's new high school, whose job was to help the daughter adjust to the new cultural situation and who was also of the Appalachian heritage and had also experienced migration to the city a few years back	

and to integrate traditional family values, ideas, and behaviors into their current social situation. To elaborate on the Socratic reflection intervention, the practitioner conducted regular informal conversations with the Graham family about their lives in their previous home area, encouraging them to remember and share the activities that helped them feel together and a part of their community. As a part of these conversations the practitioner encouraged the family to think of ways they could revive and continue those traditions with each other, even though they were no longer back home. This intervention was helpful to the Grahams because, like many families experiencing a migration crisis, they falsely assumed that they needed to focus more on doing things differently in their new home, rather than preserve what they once had.

The Graham family eventually became active at the settlement house and also at their new church. In fact, they became active in serving the function of coach at the settlement house, helping other Appalachian heritage families who had recently migrated to the city adjust to a new life and culture.

SUMMARY

Anomic depression frequently occurs during periods of migration that disrupt the person's traditional methods of discovering and experiencing meaning. This chapter has described the problem of reactive anomic depression and a holistic orientation to the treatment of this kind of crisis problem. Socratic reflection, social skills training, and network intervention are three valuable treatment activities to use in instances of anomic depression that is reactive to migration. Environmental interventions, including linkage of the client(s) with appropriate social service providers, are almost always essential. Practitioner advocacy is often required, as clients usually feel unsure about how to navigate their way through the new service environment.

12

Intervention with Survivors of Rape

RAPE IS A FORM OF PHYSICAL VIOLENCE, A SEXUAL ACT PERFORMED ON A person against his or her will or when he or she is unable to give consent (Bell, 1995). Rape has been the fastest-rising violent crime in the United States since the early 1970s. According to the United States Department of Justice, more than 65,000 American women were raped in 2004, and another 43,400 women were the victims of attempted rape (Catalano, 2005). In spite of the frequent occurrence of rape, survivors do not receive the supportive attention they deserve from the justice system, the mental health system, and the community at large (Lantz & Lantz, 1991, 2001).

Persons who have been raped can benefit from clinical interventions that help them hold up their experiences of rape to conscious levels of awareness, tell their community and loved ones about their experience of rape, learn how to master the experience of rape, and also find a way to give to the world in honor of their painful experiences (Lantz & Lantz, 2001). In an adequate community response to rape a practitioner should be immediately available to victims at every hospital emergency room. Although there has been some increase in the number of rape crisis centers and services in the United States since the late 1970s, many rape victims do not go to these centers, and many of them do not realize that obtaining crisis intervention is an appropriate immediate response to the event (Lantz, 1993).

Access to rape counseling services is often disrupted by the survivor's feelings of shame and fear, and community attitudes that foster the idea that rape is not serious or that the victim probably deserved it. The aggressive tactics that many attorneys utilize to defend persons charged with rape are often described as a blame-the-victim strategy, and many victims do not wish to undergo what they often describe as a second rape in order to bring charges against the person who has raped them (Dixon, 1979; Lantz & Lantz, 1992). Greater sensitivity to the physical and psychological needs of the rape victim still need to be developed by the police, the criminal justice system, the health system, and sadly, some professionals in the mental health system (Lantz & Lantz, 2001). Rape is a horrible crime that not only violates the victim's rights but can also result in irreparable psychological damage.

People in the helping professions should be sensitive to this danger in order to prevent psychological damage and to reduce the victim's fear of reporting the rape (Saulnier, 2001).

THE IMPACT OF RAPE

The physical effects of rape can include bruises, broken bones, and physical trauma. Such effects may include damage to the mouth, vaginal discharge, burning sensations, rectal pain, and bleeding. AIDS and HIV infection are always a danger to the survivor of a rape incident. The emotional impact of rape may include tension headaches, sleep difficulties, anxiety attacks, depression, appetite loss, bad dreams, suicidal thinking, a lowered startle response, and anger. Rape victims also report feelings of shame and guilt as well as the feeling of forever being spoiled. Additional symptoms can include humiliation and an intense desire to get revenge, about which the victim may later feel guilty because she feels such desires are bad (Saulnier, 2001). Another outcome may be an unwanted pregnancy that immeasurably complicates the life of the survivor.

INTERVENTION

In short-term existential intervention, it is the practitioner's responsibility to help the rape victim experience the benefits of holding, telling, mastering, and honoring the effects of the rape, as means toward recovery and growth. Additionally the practitioner must have the capacity to link the rape victim with a variety of physical and psychological support services, including legal counseling when appropriate. Rape crisis intervention can be done with individuals, couples, and at times families (Harper & Lantz, 1996). The following case illustrates the process of short-term existential intervention with a victim of rape.

THE CASE MANAGER

Sandy was referred for crisis intervention by an emergency room physician immediately after the man Sandy had been dating forcibly raped her. The practitioner met with her just a few hours after her appearance in the emergency room. Sandy reported to the practitioner that she had said no to her assailant, but he had insisted on having sex, raping and beating her up after she resisted. Sandy added that had been raped once before, during her senior year of college about six years ago. She reported that since then, she had been drinking too much and having "too much sex with too many guys." Sandy reported that at this time she felt alone, inadequate, and insecure. She had tried to forget about that first rape, which had gone unreported, but now she was overwhelmed with distraught feelings about both episodes.

During the end of the first interview Sandy reported that she had no sense of meaning and purpose in her life. The practitioner asked her to complete the PIL test (Crumbaugh & Maholick, 1964), which she was willing to do, and on which she scored a rather low 78 (see chapter 3 for a review of this scale). When discussing the test results with the practitioner (a score of less than 93 indicates a serious disruption in the client's awareness of purpose and meaning in life), Sandy reported that her lifestyle was chaotic and that she used "booze and sex" to make herself feel alive. She reported that she had very few real friends and that she had problems getting along with her parents. Sandy was a college graduate and now worked effectively as a case manager with children at a local mental health center, assisting in their linkage to service providers in the community. She reported, "My job is the only thing I love." Before returning home in the care of a close friend, Sandy agreed to a series of counseling sessions.

In their second meeting, Sandy admitted that she experienced great difficulty talking and expressing herself. She reported, "I freeze up and can't think of anything to talk about." She felt embarrassed about not being able to talk and shared, "I feel like a five-year-old child." Since Sandy worked as a case manager with disturbed children, the practitioner asked Sandy what she would do to help a five-year-old who had problems talking. Sandy stated that she would get out some finger paints and help the child make a mess. After saying this, Sandy smiled and stated, "Maybe it would help me to paint." The practitioner agreed and got out some supplies she could use for that purpose.

The Messy Paintings

Sandy seemed to delight in using the finger paints, and she soon relaxed considerably. She used the paints during the initial stages of intervention to produce a series of messy paintings that were not intended to resemble anything concrete. She experienced considerable joy in doing something where "you don't have to be perfect and do it right." She expressed relief that the practitioner was nondirective and didn't expect her to produce anything. The practitioner encouraged Sandy to play with the finger paints as long as she wanted. In their third session, Sandy reported that she had decided to stop "screwing around" with guys and had also "cut back my drinking." She reported that she was feeling less depression and was doing a better job at work. Sandy admitted that she did not understand how messy painting could cause such relief since she had never used this technique in her job, but she assumed there must be some connection. She also reported that it was easier to talk now than it was when she first met the practitioner.

Remembering and Talking about the Rape

During Sandy's third visit she showed the practitioner a drawing that she had done at home with colored ink and felt-tip markers. The drawing was of a small section of grass with three gravestones in the grass. One gravestone was a Christian cross, another was a square gravestone with the words "fuck you" written on its face, and the third was a small, circular gravestone with no markings. Sandy didn't know why she made this drawing but spontaneously started talking about her life in college. Her comments were initially somewhat general but soon she shared that she had been raped in college and that she had gotten pregnant from this rape. The practitioner did not know about the pregnancy. Sandy started weeping heavily as she told this story and then reported how guilty she had always felt because she had an abortion. Sandy reported that she had felt dirty and guilty and stated, "Having had an abortion makes me a baby killer." She decided at that time that she did not deserve anyone's sincere love or respect. Sandy reported that now she felt great relief about having finally talked to someone about the abortion. She reported that she had started drinking and screwing around after the abortion, and that she had previously wanted to talk about the situation but couldn't. The practitioner told Sandy he felt it was important for her to talk it out or draw and paint it out, whichever she felt most comfortable doing.

Although the practitioner was fully present and available to Sandy during these visits, their conversations were completely dependent on the client's desire to talk (or not). Many of their conversations were casual and seemingly unrelated to the substance of Sandy's presenting issue. The practitioner put no pressure on the client to verbalize her thoughts or feelings.

Gravestones and Cemeteries

During their fourth session Sandy produced a series of drawings and paintings about death, gravestones, and cemeteries. One recurrent theme that she produced over and over again was that of a small, circular gravestone with no name on it, but with a small, droopy potted flower sitting next to it. The flower was alive but appeared not to have been watered for some time. A second recurring element in Sandy's drawings and paintings was a gravestone portrayed in the shape of a cross. After numerous gravestone and cemetery drawings, Sandy decided that she needed to "name my dead baby," have a funeral for the baby, and "put a name on the small, gray gravestone." Sandy decided that her dead baby was probably a girl and named her Mary. Naming the baby was an emotional experience for the client (and practitioner), as the process seemed to make the aborted fetus come alive. This appeared to be an important development in Sandy's feeling about the first rape episode.

The Religious Drawings

After naming her baby, Sandy started a series of colored drawings that were religious in nature. She drew a series of Christian crosses and, while doing this, started to talk about her need to return to church. Sandy reported that she was born a Catholic but had stopped going to church after the rape and abortion. She reported that she still wanted to have a funeral for "my baby" but didn't believe she could have a "real funeral" until she returned church. Sandy still felt dirty and reported that even though she intellectually understood that she could go back to church, "My stomach tells me that I'm too dirty." The practitioner did not try to persuade Sandy in regard to her religious inclinations in any direction but, as with her painting activities, encouraged her to let the process take her wherever it led. It appeared that the client might be returning to some forgotten meaning that still held potency for her.

The River Drawings

After Sandy's religious drawings, she started a new series that she called "my river drawings." These drawings showed a cross on one side of the river, Sandy on the other side of the river, and no way for her to get across. As this series of drawings progressed, stones started appearing in the river that eventually made a small stone bridge across it. The practitioner, as usual, watched Sandy paint and asked questions about her products, to help her clarify their significance. Toward the end of this stage of intervention, Sandy drew a river with a stone bridge over it, with a cross on one side and a priest and a nun standing under the cross. The drawing also showed Sandy and the practitioner starting to cross the river on the stone bridge to get to the cross. The last drawing in this stage showed a cross, a priest, Sandy, a nun, and the practitioner, all sitting next to a small gravestone with the name "Mary" engraved on the face. The river was in the background of the drawing. Shortly after producing this drawing, Sandy returned to church, took confession, and arranged with her priest at her home parish to have a memorial service for Mary.

"The Kids I Work With"

After Sandy's return to church and the memorial service for her daughter, she started drawing pictures of the children she worked with at the mental health center. Sandy had always loved the children she helped with their own traumas. She decided to dedicate her work with these children from now on in honor of her daughter. Sandy had made consistent improvements in adjustment to her life since the early sessions, but she continued to see the practitioner several more times. While the intensity of her growth was significant throughout, the crisis had effectively abated during the first five weeks. At the end of intervention, Sandy's PIL test score was 126. Soon afterward, she started to attend graduate school on a part-time basis. Sandy received her master's degree in social work and began as a career as a therapist for children at another mental health center. The nature of her work changed from providing linkages, which was itself an important service, to providing therapy for children. Sandy eventually got married, and she and her husband had two children.

Meaning in Sandy's Art

As Marcel (1948) has pointed out, art and artistic expression are primarily manifestations of mystery. If we recognize art as mystery, it then becomes impossible to tell with any certainty what Sandy's art means. While this idea may run counter to the assumptions of many human service practitioners, it cannot be denied that many clients, adults and children alike, experience the healing effects of art even when (and perhaps especially when) it is nondirective. Thus, in Sandy's case the practitioner could only put forth an intuitive guess about its meaning to her.

The practitioner speculated that his acceptance of Sandy's "messy" drawings represented his willingness to help Sandy hold up and tell about her messy life. This acceptance helped Sandy to relax and enjoy the intervention process and become able to draw and tell about her guilt, her tragedy, and the pain in her life that she had used "sex and booze to cover." Sandy's artistic and verbal expression of the pain in her life, and the practitioner's acceptance of her pain, helped Sandy in her search for the meaning potentials hidden in her past and in her pain. Toward the end of the intervention, Sandy found a way to use the meaning potentials hidden in her tragedy to give to the world in honor of her dead daughter, Mary. She found her way back to a place of spiritual meaning, and in her career she was able to use her experience to help children who may have experienced tragedies of their own. Finally, it must be emphasized that Sandy's practitioner needed to be patient with her process of finding herself and resist any inclinations to take a more directive, or verbally focused, role in their relationship.

SUMMARY

Rape is a horrific event that has considerable power to damage individuals, couples, and their families. In this chapter the short-term existential intervention dynamics of holding, telling, mastering, and honoring have been outlined and illustrated by clinical material featuring the nondirective use of art. The example presented in this chapter is particularly compelling in that the rape survivor was able to transcend her negative experience and make an important contribution to her community after coming to terms with her trauma. In addition to the kinds of interventions described above, rape survivors often require assistance with environmental interventions that will facilitate their physical and emotional recovery.

13

Intervention with Clients Experiencing a Medical Illness

SERIOUS MEDICAL CONDITIONS CAN DISRUPT PEOPLE'S LIVES IN MANY ways—physically, interpersonally, emotionally, and spiritually. When a person experiences a serious and perhaps life-threatening illness such as cancer, heart disease, or multiple sclerosis, he or she may enter a crisis phase of life. It is often during times of physical suffering and concern that deeply personal questions about meaning and purpose in life arise (Ferch & Ramsay, 2003). Short-term existential intervention is a frequently utilized treatment approach when a person first discovers that he or she has a chronic medical illness, when a medical illness intensifies in danger, or when a person discovers that the illness is disrupting important sources of meaning and purpose in his or her life (Golan, 1978). Still, it is important to emphasize that not every case of chronic and terminal illness requires intervention. Clients with these types of problems may be referred to a medical social worker, health psychologist, or a medical family therapist, and their primary need may be the acquisition of new adjustment strategies that were not part of their prior coping repertoires.

MEDICAL CRISIS PAIN

A medical crisis can be defined as the outcome of any physical health problem that disrupts the client's manifestation of any or all three of the dimensions of existence, which include being of, being in, and being for the world. Medical crisis pain is the person's emotional reaction to the medical crisis. Medical crisis pain is severe and frequently not well tolerated, even when the person has exceptionally supportive family and friends. When medical crisis pain is too great for the person to tolerate, he or she will utilize rigid defense methods to cover, cloud, repress, and deny the medical crisis and its associated pain (Golan, 1978). Such defenses protect the person from the crisis pain but also disrupt awareness of the situation in a way that decreases his or her ability to work through the crisis in an effective way (Lantz, 2002; Yalom, 1980). Moving against, moving away from, and dependency are three patterns of defense frequently used to cover medical crisis pain (Frankl, 1969; Lantz,

1978). All three patterns can effectively cover the person's emotional pain, but they also disrupt the person's ability to transform the pain into healthy manifestations of existence.

Short-term existential intervention is often useful when the client's medical problem is acute, or when an acute problem turns into a chronic condition (Lantz, 2000; Lantz & Gregoire, 2003). The goal of the intervention is to help the client maintain or even expand upon his or her sense of meaning in life. Actual outcomes may be broader than this as well. In one study of existential intervention for end-stage terminally ill cancer patients in which issues of anxiety, isolation, and meaning were addressed, physiological symptoms became more responsive to medication (Iglesias, 2004). In any clinical intervention it is of course mandatory that the non-medical practitioner insist that the client get good medical treatment. The practitioner should use his or her environmental intervention skills, and awareness of the area's health-care system, to link the client with such services when necessary.

INTERVENTION MODALITIES

In addition to linking the client with medical care and support services, it is also important to utilize existential intervention dynamics to help the client overcome the medical crisis pain. In this intervention the practitioner attempts to help the client hold, tell, master, and honor the medical problem and associated crisis pain. In intervening with a single adult, it is best to use individual therapy along with a referral to an appropriate support group. In many other situations, intervention may be best provided with a combination of individual, marital, and family modalities (Lantz, 1978, 2000). This maximizes the support received by both the client and his or her family members and significant others. The following case study illustrates this process.

Mr. Barnes's Failing Heart

The Barnes family requested intervention five months after Mr. Barnes's heart attack and bypass surgery. Since his heart attack, Mr. Barnes had cut back on his time at work, stopped having sex with his wife, developed periodic panic attacks, and had become grumpy with his children. Mr. Barnes's cardiologist had recommended intervention to help the family do a better job of adjusting to Mr. Barnes's health problems and related difficulties. The Barnes family consisted of Bob (fifty-three-year-old father), Susan (forty-four-year-old mother), Robert Jr. (seventeen-year-old son), and Sandy (fifteen-year-old daughter). The practitioner met with the Barnes family on five occasions, and he also saw the parents without the children for martial intervention on five occasions during that same time period. Mr. Barnes was seen individually on three occasions.

The interventions focused on helping the parents and children become able to hold, tell, master, and honor the crisis pain that was reactive to the father's heart attack and ongoing health problems. A central difficulty demonstrated by the Barnes family was their pattern of avoiding feelings, ignoring the pain of other family members, and using repression and denial to "put on a happy face" in spite of Mr. Barnes's medical problems and limited ability to function on his job. Mr. Barnes was angry at himself for having to cut back at work and also seemed angry at Susan and the children for not understanding and for spending "too damn much money" even in the face of his decreased ability to work and make money. Mr. Barnes was angry because "they act like nothing has happened to me."

The practitioner's primary function with the Barnes family was to disrupt their avoidance and denial and to involve the family in an honest and realistic assessment of both their new financial situation and Mr. Barnes's health situation. Mr. Barnes was helped to understand that family denial was not an avoidance of concern for him and his medical problems but an attempt to avoid and minimize the emotional pain shared by Susan and the children. Mr. Barnes was floored by the amount of pain and empathy his wife and children demonstrated after the practitioner was able to challenge the family's repression and help them to tell each other about their pain, fear, and family concerns. The family eventually demonstrated improvement in their ability to handle their shared emotional pain.

Holding with Mr. Barnes

The most difficult element of intervention with Mr. Barnes was to facilitate an adequate holding environment. Mr. Barnes initially resisted the practitioner's empathy and support. Mr. Barnes had been a high-school and college athlete and had served his country as a marine officer in Vietnam after graduating from college. He reported that he hated whiners and believed that the only way to get through difficult situations was to "suck it up" and "just do it."

Mr. Barnes was able to soften up his stance and accept some support from the therapist after he discovered that the practitioner had also served in Vietnam. The practitioner was able to utilize some Vietnam war metaphors to help Mr. Barnes accept empathy and support, be more accepting of his own fears and his new physical limitations, and tell his wife in a much clearer fashion that her "tough guy" husband really did need some help and understanding. However, it is not necessary for a practitioner to have so much in common with a client in order to be effective. It is likely that this practitioner would have discovered another basis for a connection if the Vietnam connection had not existed. To put it simply, people are far more alike than they are different, and an alert practitioner can always find a basis for connection with a client. Below is an example, however, of how the strength of their connection was evident:

> Practitioner (P): (to Mr. Barnes) So you never got scared in Vietnam? You never softened up and cried when you had to write some soldier's wife or family about how he got killed? No fear! No sadness! That correct?

Mr. Barnes: Hell, sure . . . I had to write some of those letters, but that's different.

P: Bull—I'm going to write a letter to tough guy Barnes telling him how he almost died, how he might still die in the future and how scary and sad that is. I think it's a tough letter to write and it'll be a tough one to read!

Mr. Barnes: (crying softly) Okay, I get it! Hell yes I'm scared, and I feel guilty as hell. I don't want to run out on my kids and my wife. I'm scared and I'm sad. I just hate to talk about it.

P: I really am sorry. It is scary and sad. I am still going to write you that letter.

The practitioner wrote and sent the letter to Mr. Barnes immediately after this session. After Mr. Barnes received the letter he was much more accepting of the practitioner's help. Mr. Barnes reported that the letter showed him that the practitioner was "for real" and "not just talking crap."

Telling with Mr. and Mrs. Barnes

A major difficulty with Mr. Barnes and his family was their inability to openly and clearly tell each other about their emotional pain and feelings in general, including their concerns about the future. Family disclosure had been a problem for the Barnes family for many years, but the practitioner felt that Mr. Barnes's heart attack made it important for the family to change this long-term pattern of emotional avoidance as their major method of defense.

"Tickling" the family defenses (Lantz, 1978, 2000) was the intervention activity that was most useful for helping the Barnes develop a more congruent, open, and direct method of communication and tell about family pain and problems. In tickling, the practitioner utilizes double-pronged communication to both join with the family's avoidance and confront such avoidance at the same time.

P: (to Mrs. Barnes) Every time you start to talk about how scared you are for him he puts on that tough guy look, glares at you, and you just shut right up. You think he does that to help you or him?

Mrs. Barnes: (crying) I don't know! Probably both of us.

P: I think he does it to help you keep from feeling too bad (first prong).

Mrs. Barnes: (crying louder)

P: I wish he would stop it, though (second prong).

Mrs. Barnes: (crying) Me too.

Mr. Barnes: (reaches over and holds Mrs. Barnes's hand; she starts crying again and puts her head on her husband's shoulder)

P: (to husband and wife) Good! That's much better! Looks like a real married couple facing something terrible together. Good job. Mr. Tough Guy's human after all (second prong).

Mr. Barnes: (to therapist, laughing) Go to hell!

Mrs. Barnes: (to therapist) No—you stay right here! This is nice!

Mastery with Mr. Barnes

Although Mr. Barnes was able to do a good job of mastering some tasks required of him in his cardiac rehabilitation program, he was not so good at attending to certain other important tasks. Mr. Barnes was religious about his physical conditioning program (running and walking on a treadmill and light weight lifting) and his dietary restrictions. He was not very good, however, at staying away from work, cutting back on his range of job responsibilities, relaxing, or challenging either his Type A personality characteristics or his cognitive patterns. For example, Mr. Barnes dropped out of his relaxation training classes at his cardiac rehabilitation program because "I couldn't just sit there and breathe deeply and think about nothing."

The two mastering interventions provided by the practitioner to help Mr. Barnes learn to relax were cognitive restructuring (Ottens & Hanna, 1998) and instruction in the short form of T'ai chi movements (Lantz, 2002).

Cognitive distortions are learned patterns of thinking through which people draw conclusions about themselves and others, but that are not sufficiently based on external evidence. Some of Mr. Barnes's cognitive distortions included:

◆ All-or-nothing thinking: Believing that the family's situation was either perfect or a disaster
◆ Minimization: Treating serious stresses (and his illness) as if they were minor problems
◆ Mind reading: Believing that he knew what was on the minds of other family members, even though he did not ask them

Cognitive restructuring, in which the practitioner points out the client's distortions, helped him weigh the evidence for and against them and helped him replace the distortions with new ways of thinking that were more rational, helped Mr. Barnes change many of the misconceptions he utilized to "push himself hard" in the world. This process was more useful to him than the relaxation meditations he disliked, because in cognitive restructuring he felt more in charge of his thoughts and the overall process.

T'ai chi is a form of martial art that is often promoted as therapy for the purposes of health and longevity. It features slow physical movements that promote, among other things, mental and physical relaxation. T'ai chi training is intended to teach awareness of one's balance and what affects it, an appreciation of the practical value in one's ability to moderate extremes of behavior and attitudes at both mental and physical levels, and also how this applies to self-defense principles. Mr. Barnes was able to use T'ai chi to learn relaxation because again, this was an active procedure, so he was in charge and could thus use the slow movement techniques in the T'ai chi form to learn to relax.

Honoring with Mr. Barnes

Honoring is the treatment dynamic in short-term existential intervention that makes it distinctive from other psychosocial treatment orientations. Mr. and Mrs. Barnes reported at their six-month follow-up interview that honoring had been the most dramatic and important element of their treatment experience.

Throughout the intervention Mr. Barnes had struggled with his Type A personality characteristics and his great difficulty relaxing and slowing down. He reported that he felt a great need to "do something with my life" in reaction to the fact that so many of the soldiers under his command in Vietnam had died and did not get a chance to do something with their lives. Mr. Barnes felt that if he slowed down he would be failing his men who no longer had a chance at life.

After considerable reflection and discussion, the practitioner used a "guided daydream experience" (Lantz, 2000; Yalom & Liberman, 1991) to help Mr. Barnes find a new way to honor the dead soldiers who had been under his command in Vietnam. The practitioner utilized systematic muscle relaxation to help Mr. Barnes get as relaxed as he could, and then the client was asked to use his imagination to fantasize a trip to Washington, D.C., to visit the Vietnam War Memorial. Mr. Barnes was asked to find the names of the seven soldiers who had died under his command on the wall, to fantasize placing his hand over each name, to ask each name if he had the right to stay alive and then, if so, to ask what he should do with his life. The practitioner asked Mr. Barnes to imagine specifically what each soldier "would tell you in a way that was true to your memory of each of them."

Both Mr. Barnes and his wife found this experience to be extremely powerful. Mr. Barnes discovered that "all my men want me to stay alive and to take care of my family." In his guided daydream, all his men told him to learn to relax, to cut back at work, and to honor them by staying alive and not having another heart attack. Mr. Barnes understood these messages to be what his men really would say if he could talk to them. He was able to realize that he was not honoring his men by dying young. Mr. Barnes made a fairly drastic lifestyle change after his honoring experience. He became more able to relax, worked fewer hours, and adjusted his everyday actions and thinking in a way that resulted in an adjustment of many of his Type A characteristics.

SUMMARY

It is often during times of physical suffering that deeply personal questions about meaning and purpose in life may arise. Short-term existential intervention is an appropriate treatment approach in three situations: when a medically ill person discovers that he or she has a chronic medical illness, when a medical illness increases in danger, or when a person discovers that the illness is disrupting important sources of meaning and purpose.

14

Intervention with Combat Veterans

THE UNITED STATES HAS OFTEN BEEN A NATION AT WAR DURING THE PAST sixty years. As of November 2005, there were 24.5 million military veterans in this country (United States Census Bureau, 2005). Most of them served in the Vietnam era (8.2 million veterans) and during World War II (3.9 million). There are also 2.8 million veterans of the Gulf War period. The war in Iraq is, of course, still raging. Many military personnel participate in or witness combat situations, and some are tragically killed while doing so. Additionally, more than 153,000 soldiers were wounded in Vietnam, and 500 were wounded in the Gulf War (Department of Veteran Affairs, 2005). Countless other soldiers experience related trauma even if they escape physical injury.

The purpose of this chapter is to describe short-term existential intervention methods for helping combat veterans overcome these difficulties when they occur. During the years after the Vietnam War ended, it was recognized by mental health practitioners that many combat veterans experienced PTSD. This syndrome develops after a person sees, is involved in, or hears about an extreme traumatic stressor. The person reacts to the experience with fear and helplessness; he or she persistently relives the event emotionally and tries to avoid being reminded of it. High-anxiety states, flashbacks, nightmares, and angry outbursts are common. The symptoms significantly affect important areas of the person's life, such as family and work (Sadock & Sadock, 2003). Not all combat veterans experience PTSD, but some do, and many others experience residual symptoms from their experiences that challenge their abilities to function and find meaning in their lives.

Existential intervention with combat veterans is not always short term in nature (Lantz, 2002). Longer-term intervention is often appropriate when the client is suffering in a frozen crisis pattern because he or she did not receive crisis intervention after the traumatic event (Lantz & Gregoire, 2000a, 2000b). This is the kind of situation that frequently occurs after a person has experienced combat.

THE COMBAT VETERAN AND COMBAT PAIN

One practitioner started working with combat veterans who were in a frozen crisis pattern and their families in the 1970s, in reaction to a Vietnam veteran's request that he and his wife be seen privately. The veteran did not view the staff at his local mental health center as competent to work with combat veterans, or capable of protecting his confidentiality. The veteran did not trust government agencies and wished to be seen in a private practice setting where "it's just you, me, and my wife." This man felt that the practitioner could be helpful because he was also a Vietnam combat veteran. Afterward, this initial Vietnam veteran referred other veterans to the practitionre. For thirty years the practitioner used existential intervention approaches with hundreds of combat veterans in both public and private practice settings (Lantz, 1974, 2000, 2002). We emphasize, however, that this approach to working with combat veterans also applies to those who have served in other conflicts.

Exposure to combat has a massive potential to disrupt the person's ability to develop, maintain, and negotiate intimate and meaningful relationships (Brende & Parson, 1985; Lantz, 1974, 1993; Lantz & Stuck, 1998; Tick, 1989). The death imagery experiences of the combat veteran often stimulate powerful methods of defense (most often avoidance or aggression) that are designed to push people away and protect the veteran from the vulnerabilities of meanings, friendship, intimacy, and love. Tick (1989) describes this process as the "Vietnam Best." For example, Bob, a combat veteran who served in South Vietnam in 1967, reported:

I was exposed to so much death. After about six months, five of my friends had been killed. One day I snapped. I just said, "Fuck it." I stopped having friends. I caught a fucking spider and put it in a jar. The spider was my only friend. I didn't care about anybody else. In the end the spider died, too. I ended up being a cold fucker. I guess I still am. Vietnam can make you like that. It happened to a lot of us.

Many combat veterans learned too early in their lives about what Frankl (1959) described as the tragic triad (guilt, suffering, and death) and Heidegger (1962) called "thrown-ness" (the fact of death). In both Frankl's (1959) "Existenzanalyse" and Heidegger's (1962) "Daseinanalyse," the experience of death (i.e., death imagery) creates massive anxiety about interpersonal relationships, intimacy, meaning, closeness, and love. In both frameworks it is understood that a person exposed to too much death imagery at too young an age often reacts to such experiences with avoidance, aggression, and a hard shell in an effort to protect him or herself from the vulnerabilities of love, meaning, and intimacy. This effort to protect the self lies at the heart of combat attachment difficulties. Helping the veteran overcome the combat attachment disorder is done in existential intervention by providing the veteran with an empathic experience that includes holding, telling, mastering, and honoring the veteran's combat experiences and combat pain (Lantz, 1974, 2002).

Emotional combat pain directly experienced by the veteran, and indirectly experienced by the veteran's spouse, is often ignored, denied, or pushed into the unconscious level of awareness to avoid the ongoing experience of the pain (Frankl, 1959; Lantz, 1989, 1990, 1993). Holding the combat experience refers to the process of holding up the combat pain so that it may be remembered and reexperienced. Holding up the combat pain involves reexperiencing the pain and suffering that are always a part of the combat experience. While difficult, holding up combat pain involves catharsis. As the veteran is able to hold, remember, and reexperience the combat pain, there is generally a release of pain that reduces (but does not eliminate) the level of ongoing suffering experienced (Lantz, 1974, 2001).

HOLDING THE COMBAT PAIN

Helping a veteran to hold the combat pain requires that the veteran's practitioner also hold the combat trauma pain and hold the traumatized veteran emotionally as he or she remembers and reexperiences the pain (Lantz, 1974, 1993). Such holding has been described as "empathic availability" (Marcel, 1948) and "sustainment" (Woods & Hollis, 2000). Empathic availability is a committed presence to the other and openness to the pain and potentials of the other, even when such openness is difficult for the receiver. This availability often provides the veteran with support to help him or her tell the story of the combat experience (Lantz, 1993, 2000). It gives the combat veteran a feeling of really being understood. The practitioner's empathic availability and willingness to hold and share the client's combat pain also provides an example for the client to follow through with this difficult process.

When manifesting empathic availability, the practitioner does not hide from the veteran's pain behind an ardent stance of objectivity or abstraction, or behind rigid interpretation of the practitioner's role. Although the practitioner must remember to stick within the boundaries of a professional role, such a concern with role should not result in a blunted encounter or distant compassion, which will only distance the practitioner from the combat veteran's pain. In fact, empathic availability is probably not occurring unless the practitioner begins to experience symptoms of secondary PTSD (Lantz, 1993; Lindy, 1988). That is, if a veteran's practitioner is really helping the client to hold up the combat pain, the practitioner will begin to personally experience elements of the veteran's combat pain (Lantz, 1974, 1993).

TELLING THE COMBAT PAIN

Telling, talking about, and naming combat pain is the second phase of intervention with a combat veteran. Telling the trauma is helpful to the veteran for a very basic reason. Such telling places the combat experience and pain into the interactional world of encounter, where the relationship between the client and practitioner can facilitate the processing of the pain under conditions of increased support (Lantz, 1974, 1993). Telling the combat pain brings pain out of the internal, unconscious world into the interactional world of mutual awareness, understanding, and support. The practitioner encourages the client to stay with, describe, and elaborate on the painful experience. The practitioner's empathy, when genuine, and his or her willingness to patiently sit with the client, helps the client to recognize that such expressions are not only acceptable but also constructive. The practitioner's behavior demonstrates to the client that he or she will be supported through the expression of pain. The practitioner also has the capacity to normalize the experience of telling—not in the sense of suggesting that all combat pain is the same, but in the sense of assuring the veteran that his or her experience of powerful and often painful emotions is expected.

MASTERING THE COMBAT PAIN

For Charles Figley (1989), helping a combat veteran to find, develop, and utilize a "healing theory" is an important way to help him or her master the combat pain. Helping a combat veteran to discover and use a healing theory involves a process of reflection and experimentation that helps the veteran to find unique healing activities that are personally useful in processing and mastering the combat pain. From an existential point of view, helping the veteran to develop a healing theory helps him or her to find a meaning, reason, and purpose for change, and also specific methods and activities of change that are compatible with his or her skills, abilities, and strengths (Lantz, 1974, 1999). Frankl (1959) has presented one of the most heroic examples of how to discover a reason, meaning, and purpose for change in a traumatic pain situation. He wrote of his experiences in a concentration camp during World War II, where he found meaning in defiance of his situation.

There are many ways that a veteran can be helped to develop a healing theory. One veteran may learn to reach out for support to significant other people. Another veteran may engage in activities to work off the stresses associated with experiencing the combat pain such as exercise or a type of job that involved physical labor. A third veteran may find support in religious or other contemplative activities. This is very much an individual process.

HONORING THE COMBAT PAIN

The art of honoring the veteran's combat pain refers to the process of identifying and making use of meaning potentials and opportunities that can be found in the client's experience of combat pain. To Frankl (1959), honoring pain involves becoming consciously aware of opportunities for self-transcendent giving to the world that are embedded in the traumatic situation. In other words, the practitioner can help the veteran answer the question "How can you use what you have experienced to give to the world in some constructive manner?" In the process of honoring the client's combat situation, the practitioner helps the client to find and actualize a desire to promote another person's joy or facilitate the cessation of another person's pain in a way that is reactive to the client's empathic understanding of combat and the pain of other human beings. There are limitless ways in which the client may develop or discover these meanings, and the practitioner's role is only to facilitate the client's meaning reflections through conversation and availability.

Honoring a veteran's combat pain has been described as a way to fill the existential-meaning vacuum that often occurs reactive to a crisis experience. Gabriel Marcel (1948) asserts that only the manifestation of human love can overcome the negative effects of combat. To Marcel, honoring the trauma occurs through the human manifestation of availability in the face of trauma, terror, and trauma pain. In this view, honoring combat pain is both an outgrowth of mastering and a facilitating factor in the development of a combat veteran's sense of mastery and control (Lantz, 1974, 2000).

A CAVEAT

There is a danger that the intervention framework for combat veterans presented here may be misunderstood as overly linear. However the elements of holding, telling, mastering, and honoring unfold in an unpredictable sequence between the practitioner and veteran (Lantz, 2000). The experiential nature of this mutual participation is the factor that ensures that the intervention must always be a process of art.

Combat veterans frequently enter intervention with rigid ideas about how the process should be conducted. Often such beliefs inhibit the very change they hope to achieve. The constrictions that clients place on the treatment situation often serve as a metaphor for the constrictions combat veterans place upon themselves (Lantz, 2000). In this sense, the practitioner's insistence upon experiential participation to struggle against the veteran's attempts at rigidity models the flexibility that is required for learning to hold, tell, master, and honor the pain that has affected their lives (Lantz, 1974, 1993).

SUMMARY

Exposure to combat has a high potential to disrupt a person's ability to develop and maintain intimate relationships. This chapter described short-term existential intervention methods for helping combat veterans overcome the lingering effects of the traumas they have experienced. Practitioners help the veteran overcome those lingering effects by providing him or her with an empathic experience that includes holding, telling, mastering, and honoring the combat experiences and pain. This chapter closes with an example of this intervention approach.

GOING TO DISNEY WORLD

Clay was a thirty-year-old man with a good job in a furniture company sales department. He was referred for intervention by his probation officer for help with controlling his violent temper. Clay had recently been convicted of assault after seriously injuring a neighbor at a holiday barbecue. He had been arrested two other times for disturbing the peace and fighting in bars. A former girlfriend once took out a restraining order against him for alleged abusive behavior. Additionally, Clay's supervisors had told him that his presentation on the job was sometimes aggressive and intimidating. They had advised him to learn to relax more with customers. Clay admitted that he was quick to become upset and resort to fighting rather than using other methods of working out conflicts.

Clay was a veteran of the Gulf War and had participated in the ground attack near the end of that conflict. Fortunately, very few of his comrades had been killed, but he saw many others become wounded, and still others experienced severe stress reactions during the conflict. Clay had been an angry man prior to his war experiences, but this had intensified since his return home. Never one to easily share his feelings, he believed that few others could understand his war experiences, and therefore he rarely talked about them.

Holding

The practitioner made no efforts to convince Clay that he could be trusted, or that the client should talk to him. He described the purpose of their meeting and sat with Clay, initiating conversations and asking questions about a variety of his life experiences, but allowing Clay to set their agenda. At first Clay was openly disdainful of the fact that the practitioner had not served in the armed forces. Eventually, however, Clay relaxed, perceiving that the practitioner was a decent guy who was interested. The client eventually began to talk more about random topics, many of which involved Clay's complaints about his unfair treatment by others. The practitioner maintained a posture of interest, empathy, and nondefensiveness toward the client as the weeks went on.

In their fourth session, the practitioner asked Clay more pointedly to talk about what the war was like. Clay spoke in general terms, not about himself, but about the courage showed by other soldiers on both sides. He complained about how the military commanders had botched many opportunities for a faster victory, but he seemed more focused on describing the integrity of all the soldiers involved. The practitioner listened respectfully and then added, "You were one of those brave people, don't forget." Clay was becoming able to hold images of his war experiences in his conscious mind and was no longer inclined to put them aside.

Telling

The practitioner began to ask Clay to talk more specifically about his own war experiences. As Clay did so, the practitioner also asked him to tell the story of his life in general, including where he saw himself with regard to his personal goals. The practitioner could see that Clay's identity was tied up with images of the strong, athletic, dominant male. He seemed to have learned this from his father and older brothers, all of whom had a similar perspective on life. Clay's attitude was intensified during the war, where he seems to have received almost uniform reinforcement for that self-image. Still, Clay was able to admit that he was not satisfied with himself. He was tired of getting into trouble and losing girlfriends. He wasn't sure what his personal goals were, only that he wanted to escape his violent past. The client clearly had mixed feelings about his anger, however, seeing it as appropriately self-protective at times. But at least he was able to get it out. Interestingly, Clay was much more able to talk about his anger in terms of the war (where it was more acceptable) than in terms of his personal life, where he was still in some denial about its significance.

Mastering

Through Socratic reflection with the practitioner Clay eventually realized that anger did not need to rule his life, and he could choose other ways of living. He saw that he was locked into a rigid pattern but that it was changeable. Being an action-oriented man, Clay accepted the practitioner's suggestions that he undertake a structured exercise regimen as a way to work off tension and also enroll in an assertiveness training/anger management group that was available in the community. Clay wanted to use his meetings with the practitioner as a way to monitor how these mastering activities were working for him. Additionally, the client and practitioner set up other task activities for Clay to practice, in which he attempted to approach significant people in his life to talk about his efforts to control his anger. Clay felt that these disclosures would help him to stick with his goals for mastery. During these sessions the practitioner suggested that being a good soldier and a good man involved more than toughness; it also required compassion at times, as well as the ability to let some perceived slights roll off his back.

Over time Clay changed his self-image from that of a strong man going up against a cold, oppressive world to one of a strong and sensitive man still in an oppressive world but seeking connections as well as justice. The practitioner pointed out to Clay that one of the oppressive aspects of his world seemed to be societal expectations of male dominance. This idea confused Clay at first, but he later came to accept it. Interestingly, Clay chose a new self-image as a fisherman—his father's career, but with a twist. Clay had liked to think of himself as a tough soldier, but now thought of himself as carrying imaginary fishing tackle so that he could reel in others in a noncombative manner even when conflict arose. At this time, after seven weekly meetings, the client and practitioner decided to meet just a few more times, every other week, and use those occasions for Clay to describe how his new life was unfolding.

Honoring

Clay was soon satisfied with his progress and expressed that he was ready to end his counseling. Before doing so, the practitioner suggested that Clay consider some way to honor, rather than dismiss, what he had learned from his war experiences. Clay gave the issue some thought and then came up with an idea. He recalled seeing a football player after the Super Bowl walking across the television screen announcing that he was going to Disney World. Clay enjoyed the self-mocking idea of taking on the image of that macho athlete and actually taking his parents and two brothers on a trip to Disney World. He thought it would provide him with a pleasant way to enhance his relationship with his family, and to show them that he was not only tough, but also thoughtful. More generally, Clay wanted to show all the people in his life that he could combine those two qualities, which made for a better soldier. He wanted to use the vacation time to let his family get to see the new, calmer Clay. It would be a way to thank them for their support through his years of trouble. The family spent a week at the Florida resort. Clay sent a postcard to the practitioner to let him know that they were enjoying themselves.

15

Child and Adolescent Suicidal Ideation and Short-Term Existential Intervention

SUICIDE IS ESTIMATED TO BE THE TENTH-LEADING CAUSE OF DEATH IN the United States (Strasser & Strasser, 1997). It has also been reported that one in twenty adolescents meets the criteria for major depressive disorder (March, Klee, & Kremer, 2005). Depression is considered a leading factor in suicidal behavior, and suicide is the third-leading cause of death for adolescents ages fifteen to nineteen years old (Merrick, 2005). The possibility of suicide is especially great when a young person is dealing with a crisis situation.

Adolescence is time of physical, psychological, social, and spiritual change (Petr, 2004). With some cultural variations, teenagers begin to separate from their parents and exert newfound independence, and this sometimes leads to family conflicts. Physically, their bodies begin to mature and hormonal changes can cause mood swings. For some adolescents, the move into puberty can intensify a depressed mood that ultimately may affect sleep patterns, energy levels, concentration, and school performance (Merrick, 2005). It must also be emphasized that adolescence is a time when boys and girls are faced with important questions of meaning, perhaps evidenced in their struggles with values. Suicidal ideation and depression can emerge to fill an existential-meaning vacuum, in the same way that this occurs with adults.

This chapter reviews the signs of suicidal ideation among adolescents and considers some short-term existential intervention strategies to prevent suicidal behavior. It is important that the existential practitioner always assess clients for suicidal ideation and have a good understanding of what to do when a client is considering suicide (Bell, 1995; Turner, 2002).

RISK FACTORS FOR SUICIDE

There are numerous factors associated with an increased risk of suicidal behavior in people of all ages (James & Gilliland, 2001; Miller & Glinski, 2000).

Women are more likely than men to attempt suicide, but men are more likely to successfully complete suicide. Elderly people and adolescents are more likely to attempt suicide than other age groups. Separated or divorced people are more likely to attempt suicide than people who are married. People suffering with serious medical illnesses such as cancer are more likely to attempt suicide than healthy people. People who experience chronic pain are frequently at risk for suicide. People suffering with chronic mental illness are at an increased risk for suicide. People who have previously attempted suicide are at greater risk than people with no previous attempts. People suffering with depression often wish to commit suicide in order to end their pain. Finally, people who are experiencing a crisis of any type are often at risk of committing suicide.

Predisposing factors to suicidal ideation in childhood include the traumatic loss of one or both parents and child abuse or poor parenting by the actual or replacement parents (Macgowan, 2004). Another risk factor is the presence of a chronic negative family climate. That is, the family lacks warmth, fails to provide emotional security, or is disorganized with high levels of conflict. In such families, fathers tend to be depressed, while mothers tend to be anxious. Higher rates of alcohol use are also present in at-risk families. Behavioral indicators of suicidal risk include school underachievement, low ratings of psychological well-being by others, and aggressive behavior.

Escalating risk factors for suicidal ideation in adolescence include feelings of worthlessness, isolation, loneliness, pressures to achieve, and the fear of failure (Miller & Glinski, 2000). School-related behavior problems include academic underachievement, problems with peers, impulsive behavior, substance abuse (especially when drugs and alcohol are used to counter negative feelings about oneself), and communication deficits (using actions rather than words to express troubling feelings) (Harold & Harry, 1993). Within the family there is a low sense of cohesion, poor internal communication, and high levels of conflict. The adolescent is unable to discuss problems with parents or other adults.

Some immediate precipitating events to adolescent suicidality that may be of particular interest to the existential practitioner have been identified (Bridge, Goldstein, & Brent, 2006). The major immediate factors are a real or threatened separation from a loved person, and an overreaction to an actual or threatened separation. Quarrels with parents, siblings, and boyfriends or girlfriends are common. Interestingly, adolescents who have lost an opposite-sex parent are at higher risk when opposite-sex romantic relationships are terminated. Those adolescents who are alienated from their parents may overinvest in peer relationships. Isolation from significant support systems is another warning sign.

ASSESSING SUICIDE RISK

When assessing suicidal risk with a child or adolescent client, the existential practitioner should utilize several sources of information, including the client, parents, significant others, any available measurement instruments, and the practitioner's own clinical observations (Bridge et al., 2006). Typical manifestations of adolescent depression include (and all should be present for ten days or more):

- ◆ Deteriorating personal habits
- ◆ Declining school achievement
- ◆ Lack of interest in activities that were previously pleasurable
- ◆ Increased sadness, moodiness, tearful reactions
- ◆ Changes in sleep patterns
- ◆ Loss of appetite
- ◆ Use or increased use of alcohol or other drugs
- ◆ Talking about death or dying
- ◆ Sudden withdrawal from friends or family, moping about the house

When talking to a client about suicide, the existential practitioner should inquire how often he or she thinks about suicide, how the client might make the attempt, whether there is a plan, whether the person has the means to carry out the plan, and whether there are any deterrents to the suicidal thinking. These deterrents might include religious beliefs, the desire to achieve certain personal goals, a reluctance to cause anguish to another person, and a general personality quality of persistence.

The competent practitioner has a responsibility to assess whether any crisis client is suicidal and, if so, to try to help the client stay alive. It is a common practice to attempt to hospitalize clients in crisis if they cannot make a commitment to stay alive and continue to see the practitioner regularly on an outpatient basis. Clients, of course, cannot safely be seen on an outpatient basis if they have a suicide plan. Such a plan, as discussed above, usually includes a method, time, and reason.

At times clients may feel suicidal but report that they do not wish to kill themselves. In this situation the existential practitioner should ask the seemingly paradoxical question "Why not?" If the client cannot give a good reason for staying alive, he or she should be considered at risk for suicidal behavior, and some type of protective environment should be utilized to protect the client from self-harm (Frankl, 2000; Lantz, 2000).

The following clinical dialogue illustrates when it might be advisable to see an adult client who feels suicidal on an outpatient rather than an inpatient basis.

> Practitioner (P): So have you ever felt like killing yourself?
> Client (C): You mean now?
> P: Sure, now or even in the past.
> C: Well, off and on. For about two months since my dad died. Sometimes I feel like I want to end it all, and then sometimes I don't want to kill myself. Today I don't feel like it, but I feel better today for some reason.
> P: So do you have a plan to kill yourself?

C: No, I just feel like it at times.

P: So why haven't you tried to kill yourself?

C: Well, I wouldn't do that to my family. Not to my mother or my wife or my kids. I just would never do that.

P: No matter how bad you are feeling?

C: No, I won't kill myself. I just don't believe it's a thing you should do. It's against my religion.

P: So I can count on you staying alive no matter what. You can make a commitment to staying alive?

C: Sure. Sometimes I feel bad enough to think about it, but I won't do it. I don't believe in it.

P: How about if it ever gets too close and starts feeling okay to kill yourself, you call me and we will get you into a safe place, so your kids don't lose a father. That okay?

C: I can promise that.

P: Can you promise you will keep coming back to see me until we can get you over these feelings? Are you okay with that?

C: Yep. I want to feel better, not kill myself. Sure I promise to keep coming to treatment. And I won't kill myself.

P: Great. So let's keep looking at these rough feelings since your dad passed away.

The practitioner was able to directly ask and talk about suicide and found out that the client did not have a suicide plan, did not want to kill himself (even though at times he felt like it), did not believe in suicide, did not want to abandon his family, was able to make a safety plan, and agreed to ongoing outpatient therapy. This client was thus able to work on his problems without going to a hospital and did not make any suicide attempt.

ARRANGING FOR A PROTECTIVE ENVIRONMENT

Hospitalization or placement in another type of protective environment should be considered if a client feels suicidal and:

◆ Cannot make a commitment to stay alive
◆ Cannot agree to a safety plan
◆ Cannot articulate a meaningful reason or reasons to stay alive
◆ Does not believe that suicide is ethically or spiritually wrong
◆ Does not believe suicide will be harmful to his or her family
◆ Does not imagine any potential for a positive future

A hospitalization can be arranged either with or without the client's permission as long as the client is judged unable to protect him or herself from suicidal feelings or behaviors.

In many states, psychiatric hospitalization against a person's will can only be imposed for three days, and only when a psychiatrist or medical practitioner has certified that such hospitalization is medically necessary. Most states have fairly specific rules about what justifies such an involuntary hospitalization. Such rules generally require a medical practitioner's certification that the client is homicidal, suicidal, or unable to care for him or herself, or that the client is unwilling to voluntarily enter the hospital even when faced with an involuntary admission.

It may be emotionally stressful for a practitioner to arrange for an involuntary hospitalization even when the client is suicidal or in danger of hurting him or herself or others. Many young or inexperienced practitioners feel especially guilty about hospitalizing a client against his or her will. Such feelings are best resolved when an existential practitioner is able to see a formerly suicidal client who is now enjoying life, doing well, and contributing to society rather than lying in a grave (Lantz, 1978).

SUICIDE AND EXISTENTIAL INTERVENTION

Short-term existential intervention should include the following practitioner actions in responding to a client's suicidality (Macgowan, 2004):

- ◆ Being available on a predictable, regular basis to help the client process and resolve the reasons for his or her suicidal ideation
- ◆ Communicating empathy, care, confidence, and competence
- ◆ Assessing for imminence
- ◆ Offering a plan for ongoing professional help and social support that gives the client choices
- ◆ Obtaining a commitment from the client to the plan, including an anti-suicide agreement
- ◆ Reporting the problem to relevant significant others
- ◆ Following up with the client and any involved referral sources
- ◆ Carefully documenting all intervention activities

Several intervention strategies with suicidal clients may be effective and are described here.

One group of researchers tested two models for helping existential practitioners recognize the risk and protective factors involved in teen suicide and be able to successfully intervene at the earliest point (Randell, Eggert, & Pike, 2001). One of their findings was that when the practitioner simply listened to the child for about an hour (the first model), there was an increase in the client's sense of personal control, problem-solving coping, and perceived family support. When therapy proceeded for longer periods of time (the second model) and included self-talk interventions (teaching the client to talk him or herself into persisting in the face of suicidal ideation), there were further decreases in depression, and increases in the client's self-esteem and sense of positive family support. The most important overall finding of this study was that adolescents most need an empathic connection with another person to choose life instead of death. This is consistent with the existential principle of practitioner presence, encounter, and validation, as well as empathy.

An intervention model based on the work of Virginia Satir offers further hope for existential practitioners who wish to positively affect suicidal youth in making a choice to live (Lum, Smith, & Ferris, 2002). This model focuses on helping young people work through and heal past unresolved hurts and resentments they may have experienced. In the spirit of short-term existential intervention, the practitioner uses a direct interactional approach to assess, understand, reflect, interact, change, and transform the young client. There are seven areas of practitioner focus within this model. These include addressing the client's

- ◆ Spiritual core
- ◆ Yearnings (ultimate goals)
- ◆ Expectations for the future
- ◆ Perceptions of the present
- ◆ Feelings about feelings
- ◆ Coping practices
- ◆ General behavior

Through a series of questions that resemble Socratic reflection, such as "How do you cope with the rejection?" "How do you feel right now as we explore this?" and "What is the feeling that lies beneath your anger?" the practitioner and client work through the client's distress.

Several studies promote the utility of cognitive-behavioral and other interventions for suicidal youth. One group of researchers compared the efficacy of three psychosocial interventions for use with clinically depressed adolescents: cognitive-behavioral treatment (CBT), systemic-behavioral family treatment (SBFT), and nondirective supportive therapy (NST) (Brent, Roth, Holder, Kolko, Birmaher, et al., 1996). All three groups also received family psychoeducation. The CBT treatment group focused on cognitive restructuring. To adapt CBT to adolescents, explanations can be illustrated with concrete examples and should deal specifically with issues of autonomy and trust, emphasize social skill building, and attend to issues of impulsivity such as substance use, unprotected sex, and suicide attempts.

The SBFT intervention is a combination of functional family therapy, in which the practitioner joins the family to engage each member, and behavioral scheduling. The behavioral component conceptualizes family conflict to be a result of deficient communication, a lack of problem-solving skills, and family structural difficulties. The intervention is focused on ameliorating these problems by specifically designing tasks to address triangulation, boundaries, alliances, and family patterns of conflict.

While the CBT and SBFT target specific problem areas associated with adolescent depression, the NST does not target specific domains. The practitioner encourages the client to monitor, identify, and get in touch with his or her feelings through reflective listening, clarification, and statements of empathy and support. The practitioner does not offer advice or interpretations. The main finding of this comparative study was that CBT was more effective immediately post-treatment than the other two, but there were no differential effects among the interventions at a two-year follow-up.

Another intervention known as emotionally attuned parenting may be used in crisis intervention with children who experience severe depression and anxiety (Flory, 2004). The intervention is based on evidence that emotional isolation results in poor mental health; punitive and unsupportive parenting is related to negative behaviors in children and increased child distress; psychiatric symptoms are associated with poor verbal and affective communication, tension, distance, and lack of warmth in parent-child relationships; and children's psychological well-being is affected by parental cognitions about the child.

The researcher's theory is that parental cognitions facilitate or hinder the parents' empathy toward the child. There is a defined pathway of care in a family in which the parents' interpretation of the child's behavior affects parental affect and behavior, which determines whether or not the child's emotional needs are met, which in turn causes either an increase or decrease in the child's distress and pathology. This is a good example of the vicious circle discussed in chapter 4. The intervention consists of sessions for parents that include education about their child's difficulties and the negative cycle of parent-child interactions. The intervention has resulted in significant reductions in the number of the child's psychiatric symptoms and parenting stress.

Another study evaluated the effectiveness of interpersonal therapy when administered by new but well-supervised practitioners who treat adolescents diagnosed with moderate to severe depression (Santor & Kusumakar, 2001). The practitioners in this study participated in a three-day training workshop and received twelve months of weekly supervision from a clinical psychologist. The twenty-five adolescents in the study completed twelve weekly forty-five-minute individual sessions with one of the assigned novice practitioners. Results of this study indicated that 84 percent of adolescents experienced at least a 50 percent reduction in depressive symptoms after twelve weeks of interpersonal therapy intervention.

Salthouse (2003) has shown that there is a role for the meaning factor, the basic quest of the human spirit for meaning in life, in stemming the tide of youth suicidality as well as youth violence. He asserts that the existential vacuum may be the primary condition in which the learning of violence, toward the self and others, thrives. He describes a program known as RESPECT (Racial and Ethnic Sharing Providing Empowerment to Our Community Today) that has been successful in giving youths a meaningful role and restoring their sense of responsibility. In other words, the adolescents' meaning vacuum is filled when they are helped to engage in activities geared toward helping others.

As a final note on this topic, it is worth reviewing the work of Paulson and Worth (2002), who wanted to understand, from the perspectives of formerly suicidal adolescents, what the most effective aspects of their treatment were. These authors conducted focus groups and asked open-ended questions related to the helpfulness of counseling and how the participants overcame their suicidal thoughts. The participants reported that being able to acknowledge and address feelings of hopelessness and despair was the most helpful aspect of their intervention. This is quite consistent with the existential perspective on intervention, and the authors concluded that a positive therapeutic relationship and the facilitation of emotional intensity in sessions were the best indicators of successful intervention. Conversely, participants identified as ineffective those episodes in which their practitioners were not accepting or didn't seem to believe their stories of despair. Furthermore, clients can sense when the practitioner is not comfortable with the topic of suicide and is not able to validate their pain.

SUMMARY

Most practitioners will encounter clients who are suicidal. The practitioner has the great responsibility of encountering the suicidal client, talking directly to the client about his or her suicide plans, making an attempt to develop a realistic safety plan and, if necessary, being willing to arrange for a protective environment for the client.

Although thoughts of suicide can occur at any life stage, adolescence is a stage of life when boys and girls are faced with important questions of meaning. Depression and suicidal ideation can emerge to fill an existential-meaning vacuum. The competent practitioner has a responsibility to assess whether any crisis client is suicidal and, if so, to try to help the client stay alive.

In short-term existential intervention, the practitioner should be available on a predictable, regular basis; communicate empathy, care, confidence, and competence, assess for imminent danger; offer a plan for ongoing professional help and support that gives the client choices; obtain a commitment from the client to the plan; report the problem to relevant others; and follow up with the client. The existential practitioner must also focus on the client's spiritual core, ultimate goals, and expectations for the future.

16

Practice Research in Short-Term Existential Intervention

THE PURPOSE OF THIS FINAL CHAPTER IS TO PRESENT FIVE METHODS of clinical research that may be both useful and ethical in studying the outcomes of short-term existential intervention. Over the past forty years many practitioners and researchers have made impressive efforts to evaluate which intervention approaches work best in a variety of clinical situations (Lantz, 2000). During that time period, policy analysts, insurance companies, and public clinics have recognized the efforts of clinical researchers to discover which interventions should be encouraged and reimbursed by funding sources (Coleman, Schnapp, & Hurwitz, 2005). Two of the most popular research methods utilized by researchers are the *control group efficacy study* and the *baseline single-subject study*. Both of these quantitative research typologies are valued because they can indicate with some degree of statistical confidence whether or not a treatment approach is effective in producing changes in a client or group (Coleman, Schnapp, & Hurwitz, 2005). Both of these approaches utilize comparison strategies. Such comparison strategies dictate that treatment should be withheld or delayed for the client at the start of the research process in order to obtain comparison data.

Although some practitioners incorporate baseline and control group withholding strategies into their research, most existential practitioners do not do so (Lantz, 2000). They tend to believe that withholding or delaying treatment, especially in a crisis situation, is dangerous for the client, and therefore unethical (Dixon, 1979; Lantz, 1978; Wolberg, 1965). Most practitioners believe that the earlier a client is seen and treated, the more effective the results will be. Any delay of intervention will decrease the very quality of treatment that the researcher is trying to understand (Dixon, 1979; Lantz, 1978; Yalom, 1980). Another limitation of research methods that consider multiple practitioners in experimental and quasi-experimental designs is that they tend to overlook the importance of the worker-practitioner relationship. It has been emphasized throughout this book that in existential intervention every clinical outcome is the result of a unique encounter between a practitioner and client. Existential practitioners are skeptical of efforts to systematize practice into empirically validated approaches that are said to be applicable across clinical situations.

With these limitations in mind, an overview of studies that evaluate crisis and short-term intervention practices follows.

STUDIES OF SHORT-TERM INTERVENTION EFFECTIVENESS

The effectiveness of any intervention across programs and types of clients is difficult to evaluate. Every problem situation is different, and the nature of a problem (the event, the client's perception of that event, and the client's resources) is significant in determining its course and outcome. Evaluating intervention is further complicated by the absence of consistent theoretical or philosophical bases across programs. Perhaps for these reasons, little large-scale outcome research has been conducted on the topic. Corcoran and Roberts (2000) conducted a meta-analysis of the literature on crisis intervention, and they acknowledge that, while clients consistently express satisfaction with services, other outcome measures might better determine the long-range impact of these services as well as their curative factors.

Only four areas of crisis intervention are represented in the evaluation literature more than anecdotally—crime victimization, suicide prevention, psychiatric emergencies, and child abuse (Corcoran & Roberts, 2000). These are briefly summarized here. Two studies of victim assistance for child sexual abuse (including counseling and material assistance) found that parents were satisfied with those services and reported positive family changes. Three evaluations of police crisis teams (including officers and mental health workers) responding to domestic violence calls determined that the officers were able to make more arrests, and a majority of victims shared that the intervention was helpful to their adjustments. Fourteen studies found a consistently negative correlation between the presence of suicide prevention centers and suicide attempts in a variety of cities, particularly among persons ages fifteen to twenty-four years.

In ten studies, psychiatric emergency services were found effective with regard to reduced client hospitalizations and perceived mental health benefits from clients. The services were effective for depressed persons, especially those who did not have concurrent personality disorders. They further appeared to be more beneficial for females, older persons, and those from higher socioeconomic groups. A four-year follow up of one crisis program determined that the only clients who required further intervention were those with previous treatment histories (Mezzina & Vidoni, 1996). In programs targeted at clients with severe mental illnesses (schizophrenia, bipolar disorder, major depression), fewer clients were rehospitalized, and a majority expressed service satisfaction. A short-term (three- day) inpatient crisis intervention program effectively relieved symptoms and prevented longer-term hospitalizations for clients with mental illnesses (Ligon & Thyer, 2000). Programs for children and adolescents at mental health centers have also resulted in fewer hospital admissions. Treatment compliance and the presence of family support are often stated to be important factors in positive outcome.

Family preservation services are intensive in-home programs of counseling and case management for children who are at risk of abuse or neglect. They work toward the goals of preventing out-of-home placements and improving family functioning. In eleven evaluation studies of these programs, all of which have a crisis intervention component, it was consistently found that fewer out-of-home placements occur. Interestingly, it does not appear that the quality of family functioning improved in all cases, and there is not always a positive correlation between parent attitudes about the program and placement outcomes. Parents often find these programs to be intrusive. A study of a related type of program found that community-based crisis intervention for children was successful in allowing children to remain in the home and increasing family adaptability and cohesion, but only in the short term (Evans, Boothroyd, Armstrong, Greenbaum, Brown, & Kuppinger, 2003).

Because of the many noncontrollable factors involved in crisis intervention, evaluating their relative effectiveness requires a creative use of research designs (Dziegielewski & Powers, 2000). One set of researchers, writing about mobile crisis psychiatric programs, urges the development of evaluation strategies that can control for program variability, types of referrals, and program philosophy (Ferris, Shulman, & Williams, 2001). A more extensive use of service recipients in the evaluation process might be helpful in clarifying impact factors.

With the acknowledged need for creative approaches in mind, five methods for evaluating practice that have pertinence to existential intervention will now be discussed.

RECOMMENDED SHORT-TERM EXISTENTIAL RESEARCH APPROACHES

There is a major problem with attempting to do large-scale research on the outcomes of short-term existential intervention. It is relatively easy to do research on solution-focused therapy, cognitive-behavioral therapy, and the like, because they stay near the surface in identifying outcome measures (Rowan, 2001). It is more difficult to do research on interventions that incorporate an existential focus because those interventions are often concerned with a depth that some designs cannot reach.

Practitioners are generally supportive of any research process that provides additional knowledge about intervention, but only if the research strategy does not disrupt the process. There are five forms of research inquiry that existential practitioners generally appreciate. These are the *case story* study, the *transcript* study, the *base-point single-subject case* study, *before-and-after field* studies, and *grounded theory* studies. Practitioners can use these research approaches, some of which are qualitative in nature, and others quantitative, to determine if a client has changed during intervention. These approaches cannot always reveal, however, if the client has changed because of the intervention. The great advantage of these five research designs is that they provide information about the quality of treatment without disrupting the nature of the intervention being studied (Lantz, 2000).

Case Story Research Report

A case story is an in-depth subjective presentation of a treatment experience with one or more clients (Lantz, 2000). Although this form of research is primarily subjective, it is generally done in a rigorous manner that respects the reporter's ability to control subjective phenomenological errors and countertransference distortions in the story being presented (Corlis & Rabe, 1969; Lantz, 2000). The practitioner may include a supervisor or one or more trusted colleagues in a review of the events of the story to help maximize its factual basis and objectivity.

Students in the various mental health professions almost always report that the case stories that they are asked to read during graduate training are of great benefit in helping them to enhance practice skills, their motivation to continue to train, and their acceptance of the values and ideals of the helping professions. Bugental's (1976) *The Search for Existential Identity,* Yalom's (1987) *Love's Executioner,* and Kanter's (1995) *Clinical Studies in Case Management* are outstanding examples of case story presentations that can have a positive influence on the development of professional practitioners. Such reports are highly valued research projects in the existential orientation to mental health intervention (Kondrat, 1992).

An intervention was described in chapter 8 that used photographs as a means of helping an older adult client (Mrs. Norris) to re-collect meanings that she had forgotten and deposited in the past. Such an interesting and successful intervention might become the basis for a detailed case story that the practitioner could compose and share with other professionals as a research and educational tool. In presenting and discussing the details of his or her work, the practitioner might help other existential practitioners to grasp important details about the intervention process and consider some additional ways that photographs could be used as an effective intervention strategy.

Case Transcripts

In many university and institute training programs, audiovisual or audio case transcripts are used as a method of helping the person in training learn what is possible, what sometimes works, and what sometimes does not work in existential short-term intervention. Both humanistic (Mahrer, 2000) and holistic practitioners (Lantz, 1978, 2000) are especially positive about the use of videotape recordings as a research method. In this process, counseling and psychotherapy students are asked to watch the tapes of an intervention session and then discuss and analyze the session to discover insights, ideas, and intervention possibilities for themselves (Lantz, 1978, 1993, 2000). The case transcript participation report is especially useful in capturing the richness of the existential intervention process (Lantz, 1993, 2000).

It was stressed in chapter 11 that existential practitioners need to pay attention to the nonverbal elements of their interventions with all clients, perhaps especially so with migration clients, in whose cultures nonverbal forms of communication (such as the use of eye contact or silence, and respect for physical space may be quite different from those of the practitioner. A practitioner's recording of his or her sessions with audiotape or videotape can be an effective research and training tool toward this end. Watching or listening to those recordings, and discussing them in a small group, may help other practitioners learn how to appropriately conduct themselves when working with similar clients.

Base-Point Single-Subject Case Design Studies

In many practitioner training and residency programs, base-point single-subject case design is taught as the evaluation method of choice. In this process, desired outcome variables are measured in the client at the beginning of intervention with a valid assessment tool (many of these are available), and they are measured at intervals throughout the intervention. This is different from the baseline single-subject study described earlier because there is no delay of intervention in order to firmly establish a baseline condition.

Existential practitioners generally appreciate this method of evaluation and research because it can be used in a way that respects the client's individuality and facilitates the process of tailoring strategies, and it does not require that treatment be withheld or delayed (Reed & Eisman, 2006). Although base-point single-subject case design cannot reveal whether clients have changed because of the intervention, it can help to discover how much clients have changed (or not) during the time the intervention was being provided.

The base-point single-subject design may be a particularly appropriate research tool with suicidal adolescents (as discussed in chapter 15). This is because the existential practitioner must always be concerned with the suicidal client's mood and level of adjustment, and measuring suicidality at a regular interval (perhaps weekly or even more often) with a valid and reliable (and preferably brief) instrument provides a means of both measuring progress and also reassessing lethality. If the client's mood and commitment to life improve over time, the practitioner may also be able to determine the specific intervention activities that were associated with those changes.

Before-and-After Field Studies

A before-and-after field study involves an attempt to evaluate the impact of short-term existential intervention with respect to a client's concern by measuring indicators of that problem at the beginning of intervention and then again afterward to see if change occurred (Lantz & Gregoire, 2000a, 2000b). The researcher may also measure the client's condition at some point after the intervention ends to see if any changes persist over time. In all three evaluation periods, both subjective (such as client self-report or the observations of significant others) and objective (formal scales or other instruments) measures can be used to confirm or deny that change has occurred between intake, termination, and the follow-up evaluation. Again, this study design cannot determine if change occurred because of the intervention, but it can reveal whether significant change occurred during treatment. Existential practitioners use this type of field evaluation because, again, it does not withhold treatment, does not disrupt the tailoring of treatment to meet the needs of each study subject, and honors the uniqueness of every client requesting help. This type of field evaluation has been evaluated in crisis work with Vietnam veterans (Lantz, 1993; Lantz & Gregoire, 2000a), hypersomatic couples and families (Lantz, 1978, 1992, 1993), medically ill clients (Lantz, 1996; Lantz and Gregoire, 2000b), and postparental couples (Lantz, 1999).

Grounded Theory Studies

The final research study form valued by existential practitioners is the grounded theory research study (Lantz, 2000). This is a qualitative, phenomenological, inductive study approach that attempts to discover data, data themes, and emerging theory that are grounded in observation of the study population (Glaser & Strauss, 1967; Lantz, 2000). In such a study the researcher can identify a client, group of clients, or vulnerable population that has already changed and then utilize open-ended reflection questions to obtain the research subjects' ideas about why they changed, how they progressed, and why they were able to grow. Such a study can become credible (valid) through the use of qualitative research methods such as prolonged observation, methodological triangulation, data triangulation, peer debriefing, and reflection by the researcher to work toward accurate and credible observation (Glaser & Strauss, 1967; Greenlee & Lantz, 1993; Lantz, 1987, 2002). This form of study can identify natural healing dynamics and treatment methods that are particularly helpful to a specific client population and can be utilized by the existential practitioner to specify possibilities for the individualizing of intervention (Harper & Lantz, 1996; Kondrat, 1992).

Sandy, the rape survivor discussed in chapter 12, might have been a suitable client to engage in a grounded theory study. Following her desire to end the intervention, the practitioner might have engaged her in a series of moderately structured but detailed interviews in an effort to better understand her growth process. By recording these interviews, the practitioner/researcher could carefully study her words and look for themes that might help to account for her particular change process. Another researcher may become involved in the study as well to provide an additional perspective on Sandy's process and a check on the primary researcher's possible biases. An outcome of this study might be some new information about how interventions featuring art (painting, in this case) help clients with problems similar to Sandy's. The client herself might benefit as well from the opportunity to further reflect on her emotional processes.

SUMMARY

Short-term existential intervention is a treatment approach that respects and values the complexities and depths of human life and the intervention process. The importance of providing the client with assistance as soon as possible after a service request or a referral turns the process of research into a difficult affair. That is, the desire to study and understand the effectiveness of the process cannot be permitted to get in the way of that process. In this chapter, the usefulness of the control group experimental efficacy research design and the baseline single-subject study have been challenged from the existential perspective. Alternative research methods more suited to crisis work have been presented in this chapter, including the case story method, case transcript method, base-point single-subject case design, before-after field study, and the grounded theory method.

Short-term existential intervention can be among the most rewarding forms of direct practice for human service professionals. Practitioners meet clients in their most vulnerable emotional states and have an opportunity to help them not merely return to baseline but experience genuine and satisfying personal growth as they deal constructively with their emotional pain. This often (but not always) occurs relatively quickly, and at those times the practitioner can experience the pleasure of seeing the positive results of his or her efforts. Short-term existential intervention, as described in this book, is nevertheless a difficult and often draining activity for the practitioner. It seeks depth in helping a client, couple, or family face their struggles and become able to make healing commitments to people and purposes outside themselves, as well as addressing their individual hopes and fears. One of the rewards of this type of work is that the practitioner is also changed in ways that promote his or her own understanding of the fundamental dilemmas of human existence.

References

Ablon, S. L. (1996). The therapeutic action of play. *Journal of the American Academy of Child and Adolescent Psychiatry, 35*(4), 545–547.

Ackerman, N. (1966). *Treating the troubled family.* New York: Basic Books.

Aldwin, C. M. (1994). *Stress, coping, and development: An integrative perspective.* New York: Guilford.

Alper, G. (2002). Up close and personal: September 11, through the lens of a psychotherapist. *Journal of Loss & Trauma, 7*(4), 251–261.

American Psychiatric Association. (2000). *Diagnostic and statistical manual of mental disorders* (4th ed.). Washington, DC: Author.

Andrews, E. (1974). *The emotionally disturbed family.* New York: Jason Aronson.

Ansbacher, H., & Ansbacher, R. R. (1956). *The individual psychology of Alfred Adler.* New York: Basic Books.

Banyard, V. L., & Graham-Bermann, S. A. (1993). A gender analysis of theories of coping with stress. *Psychology of Women Quarterly, 17,* 303–318.

Barker, R. (1999). *The social work dictionary.* Washington, DC: NASW Press.

Bateson, J. (1967). *Naven.* Stanford, CA: Stanford University Press.

Bell, J. (1995). Traumatic event debriefing: Service delivery designs and the role of social work. *Social Work, 40,* 36–43.

Berg, I., & Dolan, Y. (2001). *Tales of solutions: A collection of hope-inspiring stories.* New York: W. W. Norton.

Berger, J. (1984). Crisis intervention. *Social Work in Health Care, 10,* 81–92.

Brende, J., & Parson, R. (1985). *Vietnam veterans: The road to recovery.* New York: Signet Books.

Brent, D. A., Roth, C. M., Holder, D. P., Kolko, D. J., Birmaher, B., Johnson, B. A., et al. (1996). Psychosocial interventions for treating adolescent suicidal depression: A comparison of three psychosocial interventions. In E. D. Hibbs & P. S. Jensen (Eds.), *Psychosocial treatments for child and adolescent disorders: Empirically based strategies for clinical practice* (pp. 187–206). Washington, DC: American Psychological Association.

Bretherton, R., & Orner, R. (2003). Positive psychotherapy in disguise. *Psychologist, 16*(3), 136–137.

Bridge, J. A., Goldstein, T. T., & Brent, D. A. (2006). Adolescent suicide and suicidal behavior. *Journal of Child Psychology and Psychiatry, 47*(3/4), 372–394.

Bronson, D. (2002). A behavioral approach to social work treatment. In A. Roberts & G. Greene (Eds), *Social workers' desk reference* (pp. 137–143). New York: Oxford University Press.

Bugental, J. (1976). *The search for existential identity.* San Francisco: Jossey-Bass.

Burckell, L. A., & Goldfriend, M. R. (2006). Therapist qualities preferred by sexual minority individuals. *Psychotherapy: Theory, Research, Practice, Training, 43*(1), 32–49.

Burnside, I., & Haight, B. (1994). Reminiscence and life review: Therapeutic interventions for older people. *Nursing Practitioner, 19*(4), 55–61.

Caplan, G. (1990). Loss, stress, and mental health. *Community Mental Health Journal, 26*(1), 27–48.

Carter, B., & McGoldrick, M. (2005). *The expanded family life cycle: Individual, family, and social perspectives* (3rd ed.). Boston: Allyn & Bacon.

Catalano, S. M. (2005). *Crime victimization survey.* Washington, DC: Bureau of Justice Statistics, Office of Justice Programs, United States Department of Justice.

Coady, N. (1993). The worker-client relationship revisited. *Families in Society, 74,* 291–298.

Coleman, M., Schnapp, W., & Hurwitz, D. (2005). Overview of publicly funded managed behavioral health care. *Administration and Policy and Mental Health, 32*(4), 321–340.

Congress, E. (1997). *Multicultural perspectives in working with families.* New York: Springer.

Corcoran, J. (2001). Solution focused therapy. In R. Lehmann & N. Coady (Eds.), *Theoretical perspectives for direct social work practice* (pp. 326–346). New York: Springer.

Corcoran, J., & Roberts, A. R. (2000). Research on crisis intervention and recommendations for future research. In A. R. Roberts (Ed.), *Crisis intervention handbook: Assessment, treatment, and research* (2nd ed., pp. 453–486). New York: Oxford University Press.

Corlis, R., & Rabe, P. (1969). *Psychotherapy from the center.* Scranton, PA: International Textbook Company.

Corwin, M. (2002). *Brief treatment in clinical social work practice.* Pacific Grove, CA: Brooks/Cole.

Cowger, C., & Snively, C. (2002). Assessing direct strengths. In A. Roberts & G. Greene (Eds.), *Social workers' desk reference* (pp. 221–226). New York: Oxford University Press.

Crumbaugh, J. (1963). The relation of Karios to encounter in psychotherapy. *Review of Existential Psychology and Psychiatry, 3,* 35–38.

Crumbaugh, J. C. (1968). Cross-validation of Purpose in Life Test based on Frankl's concepts. *Journal of Individual Psychology, 24,* 74–81.

Crumbaugh, J. C., & Henrion, R. (1988). The PIL test: Administration, interpretation, uses theory and critique. *International Forum for Logotherapy, 11*(2), 76–88.

Crumbaugh, J., & Maholick, L. (1964). *Purpose in life test.* Murfreesboro, TN: Psychometric Affiliates.

Curry, A. (1967). Toward a phenomenological study of the family. *Existential Psychiatry, 6,* 35–44.

DeJong, P. (2002). Solution focused therapy. In A. Roberts & G. Greene (Eds.), *Social workers' desk reference* (pp. 112–116). New York: Oxford University Press.

Department of Veteran Affairs. (2005). *Principal wars in which the US participated: US military personnel serving and casualties.* Washington, DC: Directorate for Information Operations and Reports. U.S. Department of Defense.

DiClemente, C. C., & Prochaska, J. O. (1998). Toward a comprehensive trans-theoretical model of change: Stages of change and addictive behaviors. In W. R. Miller & N. Heather (Eds.), *Treating addictive behaviors* (2nd ed., pp. 3–24). New York: Plenum.

Dixon, S. (1979). *Working with people in crisis.* New York: Mosby.

Dziegielewski, S. F., & Powers, G. T. (2000). Designs and procedures for evaluating crisis intervention. In A. R. Roberts (Ed.), *Crisis intervention handbook: Assessment, treatment, and research* (2nd ed., pp. 487–511). New York: Oxford University Press.

Ell, K. (1996), Crisis theory and social work practice. In F. J. Turner (Ed.), *Social work treatment* (pp. 168–190). New York: Free Press.

Erikson, E. (1959). *Identity and the life cycle.* New York: International Universities Press.

Erikson, E. (1968*). Identity: Youth and crisis.* New York: W. W. Norton.

Evans, M. E., Boothroyd, R. A., Armstrong, M. I., Greenbaum, P. E., Brown, E. C., & Kuppinger, A. D. (2003). An experimental study of the effectiveness of intensive in-home crisis services for children and their families: Program outcomes. *Journal of Emotional and Behavioral Disorders, 11*(2), 93–104.

Ferch, S. R., & Ramsey, M. I. (2003). Sacred conversation: A spiritual response to unavoidable suffering. *Canadian Journal of Counseling, 37*(1), 16–27.

Ferris, L. E., Shulman, K. L., & Williams, J. I. (2001). Methodological challenges in evaluating mobile crisis psychiatric programs. *The Canadian Journal of Program Evaluation, 16*(2), 27–40.

Figley, C. (1989). *Helping traumatized families.* San Francisco: Jossey-Bass.

Fitzsimmons, S., & Buettner, L. L. (2003). Therapeutic recreation intervention for need-driven dementia-compromised behaviors in community dwellers. *American Journal of Alzheimer's Disease and Other Dementias, 17*(6), 367–381.

Flicker, S. M. (2005). The relationship between ethnic matching, therapeutic alliance, and treatment outcome with Hispanic and Anglo adolescents in family therapy. *Dissertation Abstracts International, 65*(8-B), 4282.

Flory, V. (2004). A novel clinical intervention for severe childhood depression and anxiety. *Clinical Child Psychology and Psychiatry, 9*(1), 9–23.

Fong, R., & Furuto, D. (Eds.). (2001). *Culturally competent practice: Skills, interventions, and evaluations.* Boston: Allyn & Bacon.

Frank, J. D., & Frank, J. B. (1993). *Persuasion and healing: A comparative study of psychotherapy* (3rd ed.). Baltimore: Johns Hopkins University Press.

Frankl, V. (1955). *The doctor and the soul.* New York: Vintage Press.

Frankl, V. (1959). *Man's search for meaning.* New York: Simon & Schuster.

Frankl, V. (1967). *Psychotherapy and existentialism.* New York: Simon & Schuster.

Frankl, V. (1969). *The will to meaning.* New York: New American Library.

Frankl, V. (1975). *The unconscious god.* New York: Simon & Schuster.

Frankl, V. (1978). *The unheard cry for meaning.* New York: Simon & Schuster.

Frankl, V. (1997). *Man's search for ultimate meaning.* New York: Perseus.

Frankl, V. (2000). *Recollections.* New York: Perseus.

Freud, A. (1946). *The ego and the mechanisms of defense.* New York: International Universities Press.

Freud, S. (1917). *A general introduction to psychoanalysis.* New York: Washington Square Press.

Garcia-Preto, N. (1996). Puerto Rican families. In M. McGoldrick, J. Giordano, & J. Pearce (Eds.), *Ethnicity and family therapy* (2nd ed.). New York: Guilford.

Germain, C. B., & Gitterman, A. (1996). *The life model of social work practice: Advances in theory and practice* (2nd ed.). New York: Columbia University Press.

Gil, A. (1991). *The healing power of play.* New York: Guilford.

Glaser, B., & Strauss, A. (1967). *The discovery of grounded theory.* Chicago: Macmillan.

Golan, N. (1978). *Treatment in crisis situations.* New York: Free Press.

Green, J. W. (1999). *Cultural awareness in the human services: A multi-ethnic approach* (3rd ed.). Boston: Allyn & Bacon.

Greene, G. (1996). Communication theory and social work treatment. In F. J. Turner (Ed.), *Social work treatment* (pp. 115–145). New York: Free Press.

Greene, J., & Lee, M. (2002). The social construction of empowerment. In M. O'Melca & K. Miley (Eds.), *Pathways to power* (pp. 125–201). Boston: Allyn & Bacon.

Greenlee, R., & Lantz, J. (1993). Family coping strategies and the rural appalachian working poor. *Contemporary Family Therapy, 15,* 121–137.

Grove, D., & Burnaugh, R. (2002). *Invisible men.* Phoenix, AZ: Zeig, Tucker & Theisen.

Grove, D., & Haley, J. (1993). *Conversations on therapy.* New York: W. W. Norton.

Haley, J. (1976). *Problem-solving therapy.* New York: Harper & Row.

Hall, C. (1953). A cognitive theory of dreams. *Journal of General Psychology, 49,* 273–282).

Harold, R. D., & Harry, N. B. (1993). School-based clinics: A response to the physical and mental health needs of adolescents. *Health and Social Work, 18*(10), 65–75.

Harper, K., & Lantz, J. (1996). *Cross-cultural practice: Social work with diverse populations.* Chicago: Lyceum Books.

Harris, M., & Bergman, H. C. (1988). Clinical case management for the chronically mentally ill: A conceptual analysis. In M. Harris & L. Bachrach (Eds.), *Clinical case management* (pp. 5–13). New Directions for Mental Health Services, 40. San Francisco: Jossey-Bass.

Hatchet, G. T., & Park, H. L. (2004). Revisiting relationships between sex-related variables and continuation in counseling. *Psychological Reports, 94*(2), 381–386.

Heidegger, M. (1962). *Being and time.* New York: Harper & Row.

Hobfoll, S., Freedy, R., Lane, C., & Geller, P. (1990). Conservation of social resources: Social support resource theory. *Journal of Social and Personal Relationships, 7,* 465–478.

Hoffman, L. (1976). Breaking the homeostatic circle. In P. Guerin (Ed.), *Family therapy.* New York: Gardner Press.

Horney, K. (1945). *Our inner conflicts.* New York: W. W. Norton.

Iglesias, A. (2004). Hypnosis and existential psychotherapy with end-stage terminally ill patients. *American Journal of Clinical Hypnosis, 46*(3), 201–213.

Ito, K. L., & Marimba, G. G. (2002). Therapeutic beliefs of Asian American therapists: Views from an ethnic-specific clinic. *Transcultural Psychiatry, 39*(1), 33–73.

Jacobs, T. J. (1999). Countertransference past and present: A review of the concept. *International Journal of Psychoanalysis, 80,* 575–594.

James, R. K., & Gilliland, B. E. (2001). *Crisis intervention strategies* (4th ed). Pacific Grove, CA: Brooks/Cole.

Jilek, W. (1982). *Indian healing: Shamanic ceremonialism in the Pacific Northwest today.* Toronto: Hancock House.

Jones, J. V. (2005). Existential themes in constructivist psychotherapy: A case encounter. *Constructivism in the Human Services, 10*(1), 65–76.

Jung, C. G. (1968). *Man and his symbols.* New York: Laurel.

Kanter, J. (1996). Case management with long-term patients. In S. M. Soreff (Ed.), *Handbook for the treatment of the seriously mentally ill* (pp. 259–275). Seattle, WA: Hogrefe & Huber.

Kanter, J. (1995) (Ed.). *Clinical issues in case management.* San Francisco: Jossey-Bass.

Kondrat, M. (1992). Reclaiming the practical: Formal and substantive rationality in social work practice. *Social Science Review, 73,* 451–477.

Lange, A., & Probst, C. (2004). Existential questions of the elderly. *Archives of Psychiatry and Psychotherapy, 6*(2), 15–20.

Langsley, D., & Kaplan, D. (1968). *The treatment of families in crisis.* New York: Greene & Stratton.

Lantz, J. (1974). Existential treatment and the Vietnam veteran family. In *Ohio Department of Mental Health Yearly Report* (pp. 33–36). Columbus: Ohio Department of Mental Health.

Lantz, J. (1978). *Family and marital therapy.* New York: Appleton-Century-Crofts.

Lantz, J. (1979). Extreme itching treated by a family systems approach. *International Journal of Family Therapy, 1,* 244–253.

Lantz, J. (1985). Never trust a family therapist who is younger than forty. *Voices, 21,* 18–19.

Lantz, J. (1987). Emotional motivations for family treatment. *Social Casework, 68,* 284–289.

Lantz, J. (1989). Meaning in profanity and pain. *Voices, 25,* 34–37.

Lantz, J. (1990). Existential reflection in marital therapy with Vietnam veterans. *Journal of Couples Therapy, 1,* 81–88.

Lantz, J. (1991). Franklian treatment with Vietnam veteran couples. *Journal of Religion and Health, 30,* 131–138.

Lantz, J. (1992). Meaning, nerves and the urban-Appalachian family. *Journal of Religion and Health, 31,* 129–139.

Lantz, J. (1993). *Existential family therapy.* Northvale, NJ: Jason Aronson.

Lantz, J. (1994). Marcel's availability in existential psychotherapy with couples and families. *Contemporary Family Therapy, 16,* 489–501.

Lantz, J. (1995). Frankl and Marcel: The prophets of hope for the 21st century. *International Forum for Logotherapy, 18,* 65–68.

Lantz, J. (1996). Existential psychotherapy with chronic illness couples. *Contemporary Family Therapy, 18,* 197–208.

Lantz, J. (1997). Reflection, meanings and dreams. *International Forum for Logotherapy, 20,* 95–103.

Lantz, J. (1998). Re-collection in existential psychotherapy with older adults. *Journal of Clinical Geropsychology, 4,* 45–53.

Lantz, J. (1999). Meaning and the post-parental couple. *Journal of Religion and Health, 38,* 53–65.

Lantz, J. (2000). *Meaning centered marital and family therapy.* Springfield, IL: Charles C. Thomas.

Lantz, J. (2000). Depression, existential family therapy and Viktor Frankl's dimensional ontology. *Contemporary Family Therapy, 23,* 19–32.

Lantz, J. (2002). Existential psychotherapy: What endures? *Voices, 38,* 28–33.

Lantz, J., & Ahern, R. (1994). Meaning and the family life cycle. *Journal of Religion and Health, 33,* 163–172.

Lantz, J., & Alford, K. (1995). Existential family therapy with an urban-Appalachian adolescent. *Journal of Family Psychotherapy, 6,* 15–27.

Lantz, J., & Gomia, E. (1995). Activities and stages in existential psychotherapy with older adults. *Clinical Gerontologist, 16,* 31–40.

Lantz, J., & Gregoire, T. (2000a). Existential psychotherapy with Vietnam veteran couples: A twenty-five year report. *Contemporary Family Therapy, 22,* 19–37.

Lantz, J., & Gregoire, T. (2000b). Existential psychotherapy with couples facing breast cancer: A twenty-year report. *Contemporary Family Therapy, 22,* 315–327.

Lantz, J., & Gregoire, T. (2003). Existential trauma therapy with men after a heart attack. *Journal of Contemporary Psychotherapy, 33,* 19–33.

Lantz, J., & Gyamerah, J. (2002). Existential family trauma therapy. *Contemporary Family Therapy, 24,* 243–255.

Lantz, J., & Harper, K. (1989). Network intervention, existential depression and the relocated Appalachian family. *Contemporary Family Therapy, 11,* 213–223.

Lantz, J., & Harper, K. (1990). Anomic depression and the migrating family. *Contemporary Family Therapy, 12,* 153–164.

Lantz, J., & Kondrat, M. (1997). Evaluation research problems in existential psychotherapy with couples and families. *Journal of Family Psychotherapy, 8,* 55–71.

Lantz, J., & Lantz, J. (1991). Franklian treatment and the traumatized family. *Journal of Family Psychotherapy, 2,* 61–73.

Lantz, J., & Lantz, J. (1992). Franklian psychotherapy with adults molested as children. *Journal of Religion and Health, 31,* 297–307.

Lantz, J., & Lantz, J. (2001). Trauma therapy: A meaning centered approach. *International Forum for Logotherapy, 28,* 107–114.

Lantz, J., & Raiz, L. (2003). Play and art in existential trauma therapy with children and their parents. *Contemporary Family Therapy, 25,* 165–177.

Lantz, J., & Stuck, A. (1998). The art of working with traumatized couples. *Journal of Couples Therapy, 7,* 5–18.

Lantz, J., & Thorward, S. (1985). Inpatient family therapy approaches. *The Psychiatric Hospital, 16,* 85–89.

Lantz, J., & Witter, M. (1994). Existential psychotherapy with fast-track, suburban couples. *Journal of Contemporary Psychotherapy, 24,* 281–293.

Lazarus, R. S., & Lazarus, B. N. (1994). *Passion and reason: Making sense of our emotions.* New York: Oxford University Press.

Lazarus, R. S. (1993). Coping theory and research: Past, present, and future. *Psychosomatic Medicine, 55,* 234–247.

Lee, J. (1996). The empowerment approach to social work practice. In F. J. Turner (Ed.), *Social work treatment* (pp. 218–249). New York: Free Press.

Lee, M. (1996). A constructionist approach to the help-seeking process of clients: A response to cultural diversity. *Clinical Social Work Journal, 24,* 215–241.

Lee, M. (2000). Understanding Chinese battered women in North America: A review of the literature and practice implications. *Journal of Ethnic and Cultural Diversity in Social Work, 8,* 215–241.

Lee, M. (2002). *Working with Asian American populations: A treatment guide.* Columbus, OH: Asian American Community Services.

Lee, M., & Greene, J. (1999). A social constructionist framework for integrating cross-cultural issues in teaching social work. *Journal of Social Work Education, 35,* 21–37.

Lee, M., & Greene, J. (2002, February). *A teaching framework of transformative multicultural social work education.* Paper presented at the annual meeting of the Counsel on Social Work Education, Nashville, TN.

Lee, M., Sebold, J., & Ukon, A. (2003). *Solution-focused treatment of domestic offenders.* New York: Oxford University Press.

Lifton, R. (1967). *Death in life: Survivors of Hiroshima.* New York: Vintage Press.

Ligon, J., & Thyer, B. A. (2000). Community inpatient crisis stabilization in an urban setting: Evaluation of changes in psychiatric symptoms. *Crisis Intervention and Time-Limited Treatment, 5*(3), 163–169.

Lindemann, E. (1944). Symptomatology and management of acute grief. *American Journal of Psychiatry, 101,* 141–148.

Lindy, J. (1988). *Vietnam: A casebook.* New York: Brunner-Mazel.

Liu, H. C. S. (2004). Client perceptions of seeking counseling as a function of counselor ethnicity, counselor acculturation, counselor gender, and client gender. *Dissertation Abstracts International, 64*(9-A), 3203.

Lum, D. (1999). *Social work practice and people of color.* Pacific Grove, CA: Brooks/Cole.

Lum, W., Smith, J., & Ferris, J. (2002). Youth suicide intervention using the Satir model. *Contemporary Family Therapy 24,* 65–72.

Lupien, S. J., King, S., Meaney, M. J., & McEwen, B. S. (2000). Child's stress hormone levels correlate with mother's socioeconomic status and depressive state. *Biological Psychiatry, 48*(10), 976–980.

Macgowan, M. J. (2004). Prevention and intervention in youth suicide. In P. Allen-Meares & M. W. Fraser (Eds.), *Intervention with children and adolescents: An interdisciplinary perspective* (pp. 282–310). Boston: Allyn & Bacon.

MacPherson, M. (1984). *Long time passing: Vietnam and the haunted generation.* New York: Doubleday.

Mahrer, A. (2000). Philosophy of science and the foundations of psychotherapy. *American Psychologist, 55,* 1115–1125.

Marcel, G. (1948). *The philosophy of existence.* New York: Noonday Press.

March, J. S., Klee, B. J., Kremer, C. M. E. (2006). Treatment benefit and the risk of suicidality in multicenter, randomized, controlled trials of sertraline in children and adolescents. *Journal of Child and Adolescent Psychopharmacology, 16*(1/2), 91–102.

Marujama, M. (1963). The second cybernetics-deviation amplification caustic processes. *American Scientist, 51,* 164–179.

Matto, H., Corcoran, J., & Fassler, A. (2003). Integrating solution-focused and art therapies for substance abuse treatment: Guidelines and practice. *Art in Psychotherapy, 30*(5), 265–272.

May, R. (1983). *The discovery of being.* New York: W. W. Norton.

Merrick, J. (2005). Adolescent suicide. In J. Merrick & G. Zalsman (Eds.), *Suicidal behavior in adolescence: An international perspective* (pp. 3–7). London: Freund.

Metiteri, T., Zanetti, O., Geroldi, C., Frisoni, G. B., DeLeo, D., Dello Buono, M., et al. (2001). Reality orientation therapy to delay outcomes of progression in patients with dementia: A retrospective study. *Clinical Rehabilitation, 15*(5), 471–478.

Mezzina, R., & Vidoni, D. (1996). Beyond the mental hospital: Crisis intervention and continuity of care in Trieste: A four-year follow-up study in a community mental health centre. *International Journal of Social Psychiatry, 41,* 1–20.

Miars, R. D. (2002). Existential authenticity: A foundational value for counseling. *Counseling and Values, 46*(3), 218–225.

Miller, A. L., & Glinski, J. (2000). Youth suicidal behavior: Assessment and intervention. *Journal of Clinical Psychology, 56*(9), 1132–1152.

Miller, W. R., & Rollnick, S. (2002). *Motivational interviewing: Preparing people for change* (2nd ed). New York: Guilford.

Moon, B. (1990). *Existential art therapy.* Springfield, IL: Charles C. Thomas.

Myer, R. A. (2001). *Assessment for crisis intervention: A triage assessment model.* Belmont, CA: Wadsworth.

Nagent, W., Sieppert, J., & Hudson, W. (2001). *Practice evaluation for the 21st century.* Belmont, CA: Brooks/Cole.

Negy, C. (2004). Therapy with dissimilar clients: Issues to consider along this road more traveled. In C. Negy (Ed.), *Cross-cultural psychotherapy: Toward a critical understanding of diverse clients* (pp. 3–22). Reno, NV: Bent Tree Press.

Nelson, C. A., & Carver, L. J. (1998). The effects of stress and trauma on brain and memory: A view from developmental cognitive neuroscience. *Development & Psychopathology, 10*(4), 793–809.

Nomura, T. (2002). Evaluative research on reminiscence groups for people with dementia. In J. D. Webster & B. K. Haight (Eds.), *Critical advances in reminiscence work: From theory to application* (pp. 289–299). New York: Springer.

Organization for Economic Cooperation and Development. (2005). *Trends in international migration.* Paris: Author.

Parad, H. J. (Ed.). (1965). *Crisis intervention: Selected readings.* New York: Family Services Association of America.

Parker-Sloat, E. L. (2003). Client-therapist ethnicity and gender matching as predictors of length of treatment and goal completion at a practicum training clinic. *Dissertation Abstracts International, 64*(6-B), 2934.

Paulson, B. L., & Worth, M. (2002). Counseling for suicide: client perspective. *Journal of Counseling and Development, 80*(1), 86–94.

Perls, F. (1978). *The Gestalt approach and eyewitness to therapy.* New York: Bantam.

Petr, C. G. (2004). *Social work with children and their families* (2nd ed.). New York: Oxford University Press.

Procidano, M., & Heller, K. (1983). Measures of perceived social support from friends and family: Three validation studies. *American Journal of Community Psychology, 11*, 1–24.

Rado, S. (1942). Psychodynamics and treatment of traumatic war neurosis. *Psychosomatic Medicine, 4*, 362–368.

Randell, B. P., Eggert, L. L., & Pike, K. C. (2001). Immediate intervention effects of two brief youth suicide prevention interventions. *Suicide and Life Threatening Behavior, 31*(1), 122–146.

Rapoport, L. (1965). The state of crisis: Some theoretical considerations. In H. Parad (Ed.), *Crisis intervention: Selected readings* (pp. 32–52). New York: Family Service Association of America.

Reed, G. M., & Eisman, E. J. (2006). Uses and misuses of evidence: Managed care, treatment guidelines, and outcomes measurement in professional practice. In C. D. Goodheart, A. E. Kazdin, & R. J. Sternberg (Eds.), *Evidence-based psychotherapy: Where practice and research meet* (pp. 13–35). Washington, DC: American Psychological Association.

Richman, J. M., Rosenfeld, L. B., & Hardy, C. J. (1993). The social support survey: A validation study of a clinical measure of the social support process. *Research on Social Work Practice, 3*(3), 288–311.

Roberts, A. R. (2000). An overview of crisis theory and crisis intervention. In A. R. Roberts (Ed.), *Crisis intervention handbook: Assessment, treatment, and research* (2nd ed., pp. 3–30). New York: Oxford University Press.

Rovner, B. W., Steel, C. D., Shmuely, Y., & Folstein, M. F. (1996). A randomized trial of dementia care in nursing homes. *Journal of the American Gerontological Society, 44*, 7–13.

Rowan, J. (2001). Counseling psychology and research. *Counseling Psychology Review, 16*(1), 7–8.

Rueveni, U. (1975). Network intervention with a family in crisis. *Family Process, 14*, 193–202.

Sadock, B. J., & Sadock, V. A. (2003). *Kaplan and Sadock's synopsis of psychiatry* (9th ed.). Philadelphia: Lippincott Williams & Wilkins.

Saleebey, D. (1992). *The strengths perspective in social work practice.* New York: Longman.

Salthouse, A. (2003). Noguera's respect program: A logotherapeutic approach to youth violence. *International Forum for Logotherapy, 26*(1), 44–48.

Santor, D., & Kusumakar, V. (2001). Open trial of interpersonal therapy in adolescents with moderate to severe major depression: Effectiveness of novice IPT therapists. *Journal of the American Academy of Childhood and Adolescent Psychiatry, 40*(2), 236–240.

Saulnier, C. (2001). Feminist theories. In P. Lehmann & N. Coady (Eds.), *Theoretical perspectives for direct social work practice* (pp. 255–278). New York: Springer.

Schneider, R. L., & Lester, L. (2001). *Social work advocacy: A new framework for action.* Pacific Grove, CA: Brooks/Cole.

Seeman, M. (1991). Alienation and anomie. In J. P. Robinson, P. R. Shaver, & L. S. Wrightsman (Eds.), *Measures of personality and social psychological attitudes* (Vol. 1, pp. 291–371). San Diego, CA: Academic Press.

Sexton, T. L., & Whiston, S. C. (1994). The status of the counseling relationship: An empirical review, theoretical implications, and research directions. *The Counseling Psychologist, 22*(1), 6–78.

Seyle, H. (1991). History and present status of the stress concept. In A. Monat & R. S. Lazarus (Eds.), *Stress and coping: An anthology* (3rd. ed., pp. 21–35). New York: Columbia University Press.

Sheridan, M. J. (2003). The spiritual person. In E. D. Hutchinson (Ed.), *Dimensions of human behavior: Person and environment* (2nd ed., pp. 220–268). Thousand Oaks, CA: Sage.

Sherman, E. M. (2000). An analysis of variables influencing student therapists' and clients' ratings of session satisfaction. *Dissertation Abstracts International, 60*(8–B), 4251.

Small, L. (1979). *The briefer psychotherapies.* New York: Brunner-Mazel.

Speck, R., & Attneave, C. (1973). *Family networks.* New York: Pantheon Books.

Strasser, F., & Strasser, A. (1997). *Existential time-limited therapy: The wheel of experience.* New York: Wiley.

Sullivan, M. G. (2003). Sandplay therapy used to help teens heal. *Clinical Psychiatry News, 31*(1), 62.

Surber, R. W. (Ed.). (1994). *Clinical case management: A guide to comprehensive treatment of serious mental illness.* Thousand Oaks, CA: Sage.

Teri, L. (1994). Behavioral treatment of depression in patients with dementia. *Alzheimer's Disease and Associated Disorders, 8*(3), 66–74.

Teri, L., & Logsdon, R. G. (1991). Identifying pleasant activities for Alzheimer's disease patients: The Pleasant Events Schedule-AD. *The Gerontologist, 31,* 124–127.

Thompson, M. G. (2005). The way of authenticity and the quest for personal integrity. *European Journal of Psychotherapy, Counseling, and Health, 7*(3), 143–157.

Thompson, M. G. (2004). Freud's theory of culture: Eros, loss, and politics. *Journal of Phenomenological Inquiry, 35*(1), 137–142.

Tick, E. (1989). *Sacred mountain: Encounters with the Vietnam beast.* Santa Fe, NM: Moon Bear Press.

Tick, E. (2001). *The practice of dream healing.* Wheaton, IL: Quest Books.

Tsao, L. (2002). How much do we know about the importance of play in child development? *Childhood Education, 78*(4), 230–234.

Turner, F. (1996). Theory and social work treatment. In F. J. Turner (Ed.), *Social work treatment* (pp. 1–17). New York: Free Press.

Turner, F. (2002). Psychosocial therapy. In A. Roberts & G. Greene (Eds.), *Social workers' desk reference* (pp. 109–111). New York: Oxford.

United States Census Bureau. (2005). *Facts for features: Veteran's Day 2005: November 11.* Washington, DC: U.S. Department of Commerce.

United States Census Bureau. (2003). *Domestic migration across regions, divisions, and states: 1995 to 2000.* Washington, DC: U.S. Department of Commerce.

Van den Berg, J. (1955). *The phenomenological approach to psychiatry.* Springfield, IL: Charles C. Thomas.

Van Voorhis, R. (1998). Culturally relevant practice: A framework for teaching the psychosocial dynamics of oppression. *Journal Social Work Education, 34,* 121–133.

Vaux, A. (1990). An ecological approach to understanding and facilitating social support. *Journal of Social and Personal Relationships, 7,* 507–518.

Vaux, A. (1988). *Social support: Theory, research, and intervention.* New York: Praeger.

Vaz, K. M. (2000). When is a sandplay psychotherapy process completed? *International Journal of Action Methods: Psychodrama, Skill Training, and Role Playing, 53*(2), 66–77.

Walsh, J. (1999). Schizophrenic disorders. In F. J. Turner, (Ed.), *Adult psychopathology: A social work perspective* (pp. 258–275). New York: Free Press.

Walsh, J. (2000). *Clinical case management with persons having mental illness.* Belmont, CA: Brooks/Cole.

Walsh, J. (2003). *Endings in clinical practice* (2nd ed.). Chicago: Lyceum Books.

Walsh, J., & Connelly, P. R. (1996). Supportive behaviors in natural support networks of people with serious mental illness. *Health and Social Work, 21*(4), 296–303.

Wender, P. (1968). Vicious and virtuous circles: The role of deviation amplification feedback in the origin and perpetuation of behavior. *Psychiatry, 31,* 309–324.

Whitaker, C. (1989). *Midnight musings of a family therapist.* New York: W. W. Norton.

Williams, C. (1983). The mental foxhole: The Vietnam veteran's search for meaning. *American Journal Orthopsychiatry, 53,* 4–17.

Williams, E. M. (1994). Reality orientation groups. In I. Burnside & M. G. Schmidt (Eds.), *Working with older adults: Group process and techniques* (pp. 139–152). Boston: Jones & Bartlett.

Wolberg, L. (1965). *Short-term psychotherapy.* New York: Grune & Stratler.

Woods, M. E., & Hollis, F. H. (2000). *Casework: A psychosocial therapy* (5th ed.). New York: McGraw-Hill.

Yalom, I. (1980). *Existential psychotherapy.* New York: Basic Books.

Yalom, I. (1987). *Love's executioner.* New York: Basic Books.

About the Authors

JIM LANTZ was professor and counselor educator at the Ohio State University College of Social Work and a clinical associate at the Center for Relationship Success in Columbus, Ohio. Jim provided crisis intervention and other clinical services to the residents of central Ohio since 1970 and taught graduate-level clinical practice courses at Ohio State beginning in 1985. He authored five previous clinical practice books and over 150 articles and book chapters about counseling, direct service social work, psychotherapy, and mental health intervention. In addition to his university training, Jim was a graduate of the Viktor Frankl Institute of Logotherapy and the Cincinnati Family Therapy Institute. He was elected graduate teacher of the year by students at the Ohio State University College of Social Work on eight occasions and in 2000 was presented with the Lifetime Achievement Award by the Ohio Chapter of the National Association of Social Workers. His contributions in family therapy and trauma therapy were described as "pioneering work" by Dr. Viktor Frankl, the originator of logotherapy and author of the classic book *Man's Search for Meaning*. Jim lived in Worthington, Ohio, with his wife Jan and son Max. He passed away in 2003 and is greatly missed by his family, friends, and former students.

JOSEPH WALSH is professor of social work at Virginia Commonwealth University. He has been a direct service practitioner in the field of mental health since 1974, first in a psychiatric hospital and later in community mental health center settings. He has provided services to general outpatient populations but has mostly specialized in services to persons with serious mental illness and their families. Since 1993 Joe has been at VCU, teaching courses in generalist and clinical practice, human behavior, research, and social theory. He continues to provide direct services to clients at the university counseling center. Joe was the 1998 recipient of the National Mental Health Association's George Goodman Brudney and Ruth P. Brudney Social Work Award, given annually to recognize significant contributions to the care and treatment of people with mental illness. He has published widely on topics related to clinical practice and is the author or coauthor of five other books related to direct practice, including *Endings in Clinical Practice* (2007), published by Lyceum Books.

Index

Page numbers in *italics* refer to figures.